DIRECT SALES

Be Better Than GOOD— Be GREAT!

JOYCE M. ROSS

PELICAN PUBLISHING COMPANY
Gretna 1991

Library of Congress Cataloging-in-Publication Data

Ross, Joyce M.
    Direct sales : be better than good—be great! / Joyce M. Ross.
      p. cm.
    Includes index.
    ISBN 0-88289-782-9
    1. Direct selling. I. Title.
HF5438.25.R66 1991
658.8'4—dc20   91-7387
                                                  CIP

Illustrations by Tim Bruderer

Manufactured in the United States of America

Published by Pelican Publishing Company, Inc.
1101 Monroe Street, Gretna, Louisiana 70053

To all of the clients, consultants, managers, and staff who have made Camelion and this book possible.

Contents

Acknowledgments

In my life I have had the good fortune to know numerous people who have supported and inspired me. I will be able to single out only a few, but my gratitude goes to them all. Cathy McKillop encouraged me to go as far as possible in direct selling. Craig Paterson, although he may not realize it, helped me to believe in myself with his constant reassurance that I could do anything I set my mind to do. Dianne McGillis assured me that, yes, I had the skill and knowledge to write this book. Wes Hermanson through silly anecdotes urged me forward when the going got tough. Adriaan VanDenberg in his wonderfully direct manner told me to stop talking about the book and write it. Tim Bruderer contributed his cartoons and friendship.

My family has always been a source of wisdom and I thank them dearly: Alaura for encouraging me to think and to reach for the sky; Connie for showing me that you should pursue your individual dreams; Terry for sharing his caring ways and thirst for living; and Cindy and Chad for constantly reminding me of life's small wonders. To this day I still quote my dad's rules for living that taught me to respect others and myself. Images of Mom working full-time, attending school, and raising a family still inspire me to work for what I believe in and want.

Louise Woods, Audrey Zaharichuk, and Patricia Connor waited patiently for me to complete this book and reinforced their belief in me by becoming my business associates.

Introduction

There are over 5,000,000 people in direct sales in North America. Each night of the week approximately 150,000 home sales demonstrations are given across the United States!

The fact that you are reading this book means that you have likely become one of the multitude of fortunate people to join the world of direct marketing. Congratulations! You have chosen the type of business which has become today's marketing choice.

My first experience with direct sales was with Tupperware at age sixteen. At the time I did not own a car and lacked "stick-to-itiveness," so six months later I gave it up.

At age twenty-five, after much coaxing from a girl friend, I decided to retail Mary Kay Cosmetics. My first Mary Kay show saw me with zero in sales and an extremely red face. My next show did not hold the promise of a bright future either. Clearly, I was a sales failure. Through the guidance of a very skilled manager, however, I quickly mastered the skills required to successfully build a business. Within six months I achieved management status and brought my show sales to $100 above the company average—not bad for a woman who was so shy when she began her Mary Kay career that she needed a script to say her name publicly. By the middle of my second business year, I was driving a pink car.

The day arrived when I decided to market a superior sheer non-run hosiery directly to consumers. After hearing myself and my sister Alaura utter the question, "Why doesn't anyone make hosiery that will fit and last?" for the umpteenth time, we finally answered the question with, "Why don't we?" Camelion was founded in February 1984.

Many of the business skills and techniques I have mastered were painstakingly acquired through trial and error, and I believe my grass-roots experience has given me a unique appreciation for every aspect of direct selling. I know how it feels to be a new recruit with no experience and low self-esteem. I know which skills are required to increase confidence and sales ability. I am all too familiar with the frustration one experiences when shows are canceled or postponed. I understand the time management challenges of juggling a business, family obligations, a social life, and perhaps a full-time salaried job. The purpose of this book is to save you from some of the tribulations that I endured. Hopefully, by studying and employing the practices outlined in *Direct Sales: Be Better Than Good—Be Great!* you will be able to bypass the frustration inherent in any new undertaking; and instead, soar toward accomplishing your goals and dreams!

In direct sales you are in business for yourself, but never by yourself. Your fellow consultants, manager, and company will continually support you and encourage you to attain any target you set. I, too, would like to offer you my guidance and am inviting you to write to me c/o 3185 Glen Lake Road, Victoria, British Columbia, Canada V9B 4B7.

I wish you success in your business and life.

DIRECT SALES

CHAPTER ONE

Direct Sales as a Business: Is It for Me?

I still remember the day I decided to become an independent direct sales consultant. I was frightened, invigorated, overwhelmed, motivated, intimidated, confused, and excited. I couldn't sleep. I couldn't concentrate. I was filled with hope and filled with fear. With the myriad of emotions playing havoc with my system, it is no wonder I lost ten pounds in the first two weeks!

It is most likely that you have joined the profitable world of direct selling as a result of attending a group demonstration. If this is your first business, and you can relate to how I felt when I started, relax...help is on the way. Becoming an independent consultant and launching your own business elicits a mixture of emotions that have their roots in your dreams and in your fears. You wonder, "Can I succeed? Do I have enough time? Will I be able to overcome my shyness? What will my friends and family think? Dare I dream to achieve what I want? What if I don't succeed—will people laugh at me? Will I feel like a failure? What if I do succeed—will people still like me?"

There is a great chance that others are adding to your confusion. Perhaps one of your friends, coworkers, or relatives is feeding your fears while the person who recruited you is building your hopes and expectations. Who is right? Do you believe your recruiter or manager when she tells you that she can teach and guide you to the top; or, do you believe the person who is kindly pointing out every mistake you have made since grade school?

Welcome to the fear-excitement teeter-totter inherent in any major venture or new business. The answers to the above questions lie inside of you. *You have to decide to be successful!* You will succeed provided you follow the advice of the experts and provided that you work. It's that simple! You will keep all of your friends, assuming you do not become blatantly obnoxious about your success. And, you will make new friends who share your enthusiasm for business! You can overcome being shy and grow comfortable in your new business role.

Should you decide not to succeed, and it is a choice, you can listen to the "Doubting Dorothys" in your life. Doubting Dorothys include anyone who expresses a lack of belief in your ability to achieve your goals and dreams. Doubting Dorothys come disguised as caring relatives, friends, and coworkers. Be wary of people who eagerly offer words of caution. Overly cautious people are really afraid of their own limitations ...not yours. If you lack self-esteem, you may even be your own Doubting Dorothy. Refer to the following statements and decide if you are letting the Doubting Dorothys in your life determine your success.

DOUBTING DOROTHY STATEMENTS

"You never stick to anything."

"You can't make any money in direct sales."

"I have heard about those companies. Pyramid selling is illegal, you know."

"How can you sell products to your friends? I could never do that."

"Oh! You're going to sell that product. I had a friend who sold their products and she got stuck with a truckload of merchandise."

"Oh I knew a lady who sold those things. She was so pushy."

"You'll never make any money running a business from your home."

"You're not a salesperson!"

"You're going to sell encyclopedias? You never finished high school!"

"What about your real job? How can you do both?"

"My husband would have a cow if I did something like that! Are you certain you are doing the right thing?"

"Don't ask me to have a party for you. I hate those things."

"You're selling ABC cosmetics? My mother is allergic to their skin care. She broke out in a rash that lasted for three weeks. You should have seen her skin."

"I don't care what you do, as long as you don't neglect your family!"

"You're going into business again? Are you sure that is wise?"

"I hope this works out for you. Nothing else seems to have been your cup of tea."

"Be careful of what you are getting into."

Don't be surprised if some of these Doubting Dorothy statements sound like the advice you just received from a friend. People don't mean to be cruel...they are merely voicing their own fears. It is natural for the people who love you to try to protect you.

When you were a child, think of how often your mother told you to be careful. Your mother was expressing her love for you and her fear that you might get hurt. If she said it often enough, you may have wondered if your mother believed that you were totally incapable of handling life.

The same principle applies when your friends make discouraging remarks regarding your new business. For some Doubting Dorothys, the motivating factor is a fear that should you become successful, you may not have time for them. Others are displaying a selfish need to make certain no one else succeeds. Let's face it...some people are motivated by jealousy. Unfortunately, some individuals may want to control you. The need to control others is the result of insecurity. Controlling people need reassurance that although you intend to pursue your own goals, you still love them. Regardless, the influence Doubting Dorothys have over your life is up to you!

Place your trust in people who believe in you! Your manager's or recruiter's belief in you stems from the positive qualities she sees in your personality. She is not biased by any past mistakes you may have made. When your direct sales manager promises to teach you how to be successful, she is speaking from experience. Having once been a new recruit and having mastered direct sales, your manager can provide quality business guidance. Your manager knows what it takes to be successful and she sees those attributes in you. One thing is for certain, your manager would not devote time and energy training you if she did not believe you have the ability to succeed. Think for a moment. Most direct sales companies pay their managers a commission which is based on their teams' wholesale production. Why would your manager spend time training and motivating you if she did not believe that you have the talent to succeed? The fact that your manager's income depends on your success should be very comforting to you.

SUCCESS POTENTIAL QUIZ

Successful people possess common qualities and are: self-motivated, energetic, positive thinking, eager to learn, open to new ideas, confident, solution oriented and determined, capable communicators,

willing to lead, and personable. Take the following quiz to determine which of these characteristics you already possess.

Self-Motivated

Answer the following statements with true or false.

_____ As an employee, I sometimes have to be asked more than once to complete an assignment.

_____ I seldom pay my telephone and water bills until I receive disconnection notices.

_____ I always wait until the last minute to buy gifts for special occasions.

_____ When I need to make an appointment that I am dreading, I generally put it off until the very last possible moment.

_____ If I were to compile a list of tasks that I have been avoiding, my list would total more than ten things.

Energetic

Check all of the statements which you feel describe you.

_____ I have the most energy when I first wake up in the morning.

_____ I am easily talked into an evening on the town.

_____ I spend very few of my evenings watching television.

_____ I am actively involved in one or more sports.

_____ I spend two or more evenings a week doing a non-work-related activity that takes me out of my home.

_____ I have one or more hobbies that I do for pleasure.

_____ I am involved in volunteer work.

_____ I like to be creative.

_____ I have an abundance of energy.

Positive Thinking

Answer the following statements with true or false.

_____ I believe there is always a solution to a problem.

_____ People are inherently good.

_____ People are in charge of their own destiny.

_____ Most of my friends are trustworthy.

_____ I believe that love is one of the greatest gifts you can give or receive.

_____ I believe people can accomplish anything they believe they can accomplish.

_____ I believe that your attitude often determines your outcome.

Eager to Learn

Q. #1

Check the answer that best describes you.

A. _____ I love to read.

B. _____ I read only what is absolutely necessary.

C. _____ I read to gain knowledge.

Q. #2

Check the answer that best describes you.

A. _____ I often think of taking a night school course.

B. _____ I am enrolled in a night school course right now.

C. _____ I do not have the time to take a night school course.

D. _____ I have taken night school courses in the recent past.

Q. #3

Answer the following statements with true or false.

_____ People are a great source of information.

_____ You can learn by watching others.

_____ You can learn by trial and error.

_____ Knowledge is power.

_____ Learning is fun.

_____ You are never too old to learn.

Open to New Ideas

Q. #1

Which of the following statements best describes you?

A. _____ I welcome change.

B. _____ I like everything to be in its place.

C. _____ Change makes me uneasy.

Q. #2

Choose your most likely response to the following situation.

When a friend suggests we do something different for a change . . .

A. _____ I make an excuse as to why I can't do what is being suggested.

B. _____ I reluctantly agree to try the new activity.

C. _____ I welcome the challenge of a new adventure.

Q. #3

My ideal annual vacation would be . . .

A. _____ To somewhere exotic and adventuresome.

B. _____ To visit my family.

C. _____ A week in a cabin by the lake.

D. _____ To stay in town and rest.

Confident

Q. #1

Mark the answer that most describes how you would react in the following situation.

In the company of a group of friends, when someone asks me for my opinion on a topic that I am familiar with...

A. _____ I willingly state what I honestly feel.

B. _____ I make a comment that I feel is in keeping with how I imagine everyone else thinks.

C. _____ I decline comment saying that I have not really thought about it.

Q. #2

Answer the following questions with true or false.

_____ I like myself.

_____ I like most people I meet.

_____ I am good at five or more things.

_____ I could make a list of ten or more things that I like about myself.

_____ I am a good friend.

_____ I am a valuable employee.

_____ In general, I like my personal appearance.

_____ I take care always to look my best.

_____ When I meet someone new, I make a good first impression.

_____ I find it easy to make new friends.

Solution Oriented and Determined

Q. #1

Check the statement that best describes you.

When confronted with a problem...

A. _____ I welcome the challenge to find a solution.

B. _____ I act like an ostrich and stick my head in the sand until some-one else finds a solution or the problem goes away.

C. _____ I believe a solution will be found and do the best that I can until I find an answer.

Q. #2

After trying unsuccessfully to solve a problem on my own...

A. _____ I seek the advice of friends or experts.

B. _____ I give up. It wasn't that important anyway.

C. _____ I get more determined than ever to find an answer.

Communication Skills

Q. #1

Which statement best describes you?

A. _____ I am a good listener.

B. _____ I am an average listener.

C. _____ I often have to ask people to repeat themselves.

Q. #2

Which statement best describes how you would react?

When a friend asks me for advice...

A. _____ I welcome the chance to tell her what I feel.

B. _____ I ask her how she feels and what she thinks she should do about the situation.

C. _____ No one ever asks me for advice.

Q. #3

In conversation with a group of friends...

A. _____ I generally listen and respond to the topics being discussed.

B. _____ I am mostly quiet, but I do listen.

C. _____ I find myself drifting away. What they are saying doesn't interest me.

Willing to Lead

Q. #1

Which statement best describes you?

A. _____ People like me and often ask for my opinion.

B. _____ Nobody wants my opinion.

C. _____ I avoid giving my opinion.

Q. #2

Check off all of the statements that apply to you.

_____ I am outgoing.

_____ I am an organizer.

_____ People seek my guidance.

_____ People always ask for my help.

_____ When a job needs to be done, I generally offer my services.

_____ I enjoy working with people.

Personable

Check the answer that best describes you.

A. _____ In general, most people like me and I like people.

B. _____ I have very few friends.

C. _____ I avoid people.

Before you begin to analyze your results, remember that no matter what your score is today, your direct sales business will help you to develop and grow. Direct sales managers will tell you that one of the most rewarding factors of their job is watching their team members prosper personally and professionally.

When I started in direct sales I was absolutely the shyest, most intimidated, and most scared person on our team. I was so terrified of speaking in a group that I needed a script to help me remember my name. Whenever my manager called upon me for my opinion, or to give me praise, I would shake like a leaf, turn bright red, and my hands would sweat. I was so nervous that people referred to me as "Little Joy Ross." Now, I am five feet nine inches tall and I weigh about 145 pounds. I am not little! They called me little because I was incredibly shy and nervous. Today, I am thankful to report, I am substantially more confident and poised.

SUCCESS POTENTIAL QUIZ ANALYSIS

Self-Motivated

(Possible score: 25 points. Your score: _____.)

Give yourself five points for every question you answered as false. Self-motivated people make a point of doing things on time. If you are weak in this area, try working with a daily list of priorities. In this way, you can give attention to the things on which you need to concentrate and break your procrastination habit. (For additional information on time management, turn to Chapter 10.)

Energetic

(Possible score: 45 points. Your score: _____.)

Give yourself five points for each statement you marked that describes you. Most people have sufficient energy to work forty hours per week and participate in extracurricular activities. Therefore, most people can work full-time and manage a part-time business. If you are weak in this area, you may find the stimulation of a new business very invigorating. A change in responsibilities often increases one's energy tenfold. Other ideas for improving your energy level include: exercising, taking vitamins, not eating after eight in the evening, and avoiding coffee after three in the afternoon. If you are experiencing a serious lack of energy, consult your doctor.

Positive Thinking

(Possible score: 35 points. Your score: _____.)

Give yourself five points for every question you answered as being true. New experiences elicit new problems and how you view these challenges will directly affect your ability to solve and overcome them. Positive-thinking business people believe they will succeed and do whatever is required to assure their success. They are committed to succeeding!

If you scored poorly in this section, don't worry. You can learn to think positively. Negative thinking is a choice, just as positive thinking is a choice. Your manager can help you develop a positive attitude. The latter part of this book explores ways to improve your attitude. Numerous self-help books on the power of thinking positively are available and are listed in the back of this book. Whether or not you already possess a positive attitude, I recommend reading motivational books for a minimum of fifteen minutes per day.

Eager to Learn

(Possible score: 40 points. Your score: _____.)

Q. #1. Give yourself five points if you chose answer *A* or *C.* Generally, people who enjoy reading are well informed. (To ensure your success in direct selling, make certain you read your company training manuals from front to back; they contain the advice of the experts.)

Q. #2. Give yourself five points if you chose answer *A, B,* or *D.* Night school courses are a great way to improve your knowledge and indicate your eagerness for self-improvement. Your company weekly success meetings are equally beneficial. Make certain you commit to attending as many as possible. The rewards will include increased self-esteem, knowledge, and income.

Q. #3. Give yourself five points for each answer you marked as being true. An awareness of the numerous sources of knowledge is crucial for continual growth. A healthy attitude toward learning is equally beneficial. Knowledge is fun and enhances your personal power. And it is true, you are never too old to learn.

Open to New Ideas

(Possible score: 20 points. Your score: _____.)

Q. #1. Give yourself five points if you checked *A.* People who welcome change are generally open to ideas that differ from their own. If you answered *B* or *C,* you may have become a little set in your ways. An attitude of wanting "everything in its place" is fine only when your world is totally satisfying. Change makes everyone somewhat uneasy, so relax and try to discover the personal growth and opportunity inherent in all change. Look for the magic in new things.

Q. #2. Give yourself five points for answering *B* and ten points for answering *C.* People who are open to new ideas are continually tackling the unfamiliar. Although they may experience a degree of fear and are aware of possible difficulties, they rise to the challenge...some with welcome anticipation of the unknown. Don't worry if you answered *A.* You are merely experiencing the hazards of a well-established comfort zone. Make a point of incorporating new things and experiences into your life. Start gradually, and before you know it, you'll find your life becoming continually more exciting and rewarding.

Q. #3. Ideal vacations are a personal matter and often reflect one's inner dreams and ambitions. Give yourself five points for responding to statements *A* or *C.* You are open to new experiences. Give yourself five points if you responded to *B* and your family lives far enough away that a vacation with them is truly a luxury. If you responded *D,* stay home and rest, take another look. Is staying home your ideal vacation or do you need a rest?

Confident

(Possible score: 55 points. Your score: _____.)

Q. #1. Give yourself five points if you answered *A.* Stating what you honestly feel indicates that you value yourself and your opinions. A sense of self-worth is imperative to success. Without a healthy self-image, people become consumed by fears and inhibitions, rarely reaping all the happiness to which they are entitled. So congratulations, you are able to express what you truly feel! If you answered *B* or *C,* you will need to work on your confidence level. As you overcome new challenges, your direct sales business will help to increase your self-esteem. And, remember, your willingness to do the unfamiliar is an accomplishment in itself!

Q. #2. Give yourself five points for every statement you checked as being true. Confident people value themselves and others. If you scored poorly in this section, make a promise to immediately start improving the way you feel about yourself. Chapter 8 outlines strategies for increased confidence. At the back of this book, I have recommended a few self-help books on learning to love yourself. Read them!

Solution Oriented and Determined

(Possible score: 10 points. Your score: _____.)

Q. #1. Give yourself five points for responding with A or C. You have a positive approach to problem solving and will easily discover solutions for challenges that come your way. Problems are inherent in every task we undertake and alone do not prevent the realization of goals. One's attitude, determination, and problem-solving ability are the predominant factors in the accomplishment of any goal. When you believe a solution to a problem can be found, you will find a solution. Challenges are meant to be overcome, not to stymie action. If you answered B, you have not discovered your own personal power; perhaps you are lacking confidence and experience. Start looking for solutions to problems and you will be amazed by your ability to find them.

Q. #2. Give yourself five points for answering A or C. When confronted with a problem you cannot readily find a solution to, it often helps to seek the advice of friends or experts. Of course, remaining determined to find a solution is imperative to successful problem solving! If you answered B, that you give up because it wasn't that important anyway, you are denying yourself many accomplishments and pleasures. The next time you are challenged, shift your attitude toward finding solutions and begin experiencing your own personal power.

Communication Skills

(Possible score: 20 points. Your score _____.)

Q. #1. Give yourself ten points for an A answer and five points for a B answer. Most people know whether they are good or average listeners. Good listeners are genuinely interested in what others have to say. They realize the therapeutic value of being heard, and take the time to truly hear what others say. If you answered C, that you often have to ask others to repeat what they have said, you need to practice listening. By doing so, you will begin to connect with those around you. Remember, when listening, you do not have to agree with the speaker; your goal is simply to hear what is being said.

Q. #2. Give yourself five points for a B response. People who ask for advice generally know how they feel and what action they should take.

Their purpose in asking you for your opinion is to seek reassurance and support, or clarify mixed feelings. The best way to support someone is to encourage her to do what she feels is right. If you answered *A* or *C*, you need to practice listening and encouraging others to find the answers within themselves.

Q. #3. Give yourself five points for an *A* response. Communication involves listening and, when appropriate, responding. If you answered *B*, that you like to listen but are mostly quiet, you are denying yourself your right to express who you are. Listening to a friend in need is different from continually withholding your opinions. Everyone deserves to be heard. To be heard you need to speak up. If you answered *C*, that you are disinterested in the conversation, start reaching out to people and state what you feel and think.

Willing to Lead

(Possible score: 35 points. Your score: _____.)

Q. #1. Give yourself five points for an *A* answer. When people ask for your opinion, they value what you believe and think. And, being able to share your opinion indicates that you are confident. Congratulations! If you answered *B*, nobody wants your opinion, you are probably underestimating your worth and need to work on your self-esteem level. People often mistake someone who is shy or insecure as being disinterested or withdrawn. Start letting people know that you are interested and value them. If you answered *C*, that you avoid giving your opinion, stop and think for a moment. Denying yourself the right to express what you feel during general conversation or when decisions are being made that affect you, shows a lack of belief in yourself and in others.

Q. #2. Give yourself five points for every answer you checked. Outgoing individuals are generally good leaders. The ability to organize is crucial for effective leadership. If people are always asking for your help, they see you as a leader. People who describe themselves as good at working with others realize the value of teamwork. They know how to create an environment which encourages everyone to work together. Capable leaders make excellent business people and direct sales managers, so congratulations if you scored high on this section.

If your leadership score is lower than you would like, don't worry. One of the many benefits of a direct sales business is the growth you will gain as you master new skills and overcome challenges. Just by reading this book, you are already on your way to being a more confident, capable person!

Personable

(Possible score: 10 points. Your score: _____.)

Give yourself ten points if you answered *A*. People who enjoy others and see themselves as "likeable" prosper in direct marketing. If you answered *B*, that you have few friends, you may want to use your business as a vehicle to meet people and establish new friends. If you answered *C*, you avoid people, perhaps your business will help you to overcome this tendency. Regardless of whether you are shy or insecure, everyone benefits from reaching out to others. Make a decision to enjoy life more and start making friends today!

SUCCESS POTENTIAL QUIZ FINAL ANALYSIS

Self-motivated .... Your score _____ (25 points possible.)

Energetic............................. Your score _____ (45 points possible.)

Positive thinking .... Your score _____ (35 points possible.)

Eager to learn .... Your score _____ (40 points possible.)

Open to new ideas................ Your score _____ (20 points possible.)

Confident............................. Your score _____ (55 points possible.)

Solution oriented and
    determined .... Your score _____ (10 points possible.)

Communication skills .... Your score _____ (20 points possible.)

Willing to lead .... Your score _____ (35 points possible.)

Personable .... Your score _____ (10 points possible.)

Your final score _____ (295 points possible.)

If you scored 225 points or over:

Congratulations! You are capable of succeeding at everything you tackle. You are truly self-motivated, energetic, positive thinking, eager to learn, open to new ideas, confident, a good communicator, willing to lead, and personable. You are undoubtedly getting the most from life and everything you do. Your direct sales business will provide you the opportunity to enjoy the fruits of your talents. We will see you at the top!

If you scored between 220 points and 175 points:

Welcome to the world of choice! You possess the attributes necessary to success; however, you are holding yourself back. The question becomes, "Why would you settle for less than what you are capable of doing and entitled to having?" Many people hold themselves back because they are afraid; others simply have poor work habits. Discover what it is that is holding you back and vow to overcome those fears and habits. You do not lack ability, so decide to start winning and attaining new heights. By doing so you will be on the road to a future of happiness and success.

If you scored under 175 points:

Remember, in direct sales, it does not matter where you start, it is where you finish that counts! Had I taken this test when I began my career in marketing, I would have scored incredibly lower than I would today. Direct sales was the vehicle for my personal growth. Before I discovered the challenges, successes, and joys of selling I was a woman without direction, belief, and confidence. Today I am continually tackling new challenges and developing personally and professionally. Put your fears and inhibitions aside, and take a giant move toward your own happy future. One step at a time, take a walk down the road to self-fulfillment.

IT DOES NOT MATTER WHERE YOU START; IT IS WHERE YOU FINISH THAT COUNTS!

As a salesperson, manager, and business owner, I have enjoyed knowing a variety of people in direct marketing. Direct sales people (also known as "consultants") come from varying backgrounds and include: teachers, nurses, housewives, students, investment brokers, secretaries, accountants, professional singers, hairdressers, social workers, travel agents, artists, and the list goes on. Some of the direct sales people I have met are confident and gregarious; others are shy and self-conscious. Some are brilliant, others talented. Some are short, many are of average height, and some are tall. Some are physically fit, others handicapped. Some consultants find learning easy and fun, others have to be taught numerous times before they fully grasp a new concept or skill. Some consultants begin their businesses with preset goals, others must learn how to set goals. Some are well dressed; some own one business outfit. Some are accomplished speakers; many are terrified by the prospect of conducting their first group demonstration. In fact, the only "common" attribute among the numerous direct sales people I have met is their uniqueness!

It is also a fact that the past experiences, skills, abilities, attributes, and personalities of those who rise to the top in direct sales varies considerably. What those who succeed do have in common is a willingness to learn the art of direct selling and to practice what they learn. And, selling is an art!

I remember the beginning of my own direct selling career. I was confident that I would succeed. In fact, against the advice of my sales manager, I had even quit my full-time job so that I could totally concentrate on my new business. I was excited and filled with hope and energy. My future looked promising. At least it did until I tackled my first group sales demonstration.

Under the watchful and protective eye of my father, I loaded $2,000 worth of skin care products and makeup into my family's vehicle. "Do you think you will need all of that?" my father asked as I carted the last suitcase to the Ramcharger he had graciously loaned me. Immediately I was defensive. Surely a woman's family should have more faith. "Yes, I will!" came my naive reply. "I need to have a variety of products. There will be six guests at the show." I quickly dismissed my dad's comments and set out to make my first big sale.

I could hardly wait to begin. I was already counting the profit I would make. My makeup was applied expertly and the one and only professional business outfit I owned had been dry-cleaned for the occasion. I was convinced that everyone would be as excited about Mary Kay Cosmetics as I was. And they were. Throughout my presentation they nodded their heads in agreement as I explained the importance of caring for your skin and suggested new techniques for applying eye shadow and blush. I had them...until...the close! Suddenly, all of my confidence was gone. How could I ask people to give me their money? Oh, no! I couldn't! I hung my head, folded my hands in front of me, and said, "If anybody thinks they want anything, let me know." I left the table and waited.

As you can well imagine, with my less than powerful close, my sales that evening were zero. Where had I gone wrong? They had all been impressed with my presentation and products. Simple! I had lost my nerve at the close and had acted embarrassed and guilty. My fear of asking for something, especially other people's money, had been interpreted as a lack of confidence in my products, not in myself, as was really the case. Looking back, my hostess and her guests must have wondered why I was selling a product that I didn't truly believe was the best available. After all, if I believed everyone should be wearing Mary Kay skin care and cosmetics, I should have cemented my conviction with a confident close!

Anyone who knows me will attest to the fact that I will only market superior products. I believed in my products, I had been using Mary Kay for a couple of years, and I certainly would not have quit my full-time job to market a product in which I did not have total confidence. My problem was a lack of confidence in my own self-worth, not my products. What I needed to learn was that when you truly believe in the products you market, you should never feel awkward about encouraging others to use those products. The fact that my friends would need to part with their money to attain the extraordinary benefits of Mary Kay skin care was a fact of economics, not my greed. And, if my friends were not using Mary Kay, they would likely end up buying another product line which may not have been as effective. In short, I owed it to my friends to be honest and encourage them to buy a product I knew in my heart was the best!

From the above story, you can see that I had many important lessons to learn when I began my direct sales career. From my first show, my sales gradually grew. Within three months I was surpassing the average Mary Kay show sales by $100, but not before I learned to think of my clients first and my own insecurities second. When I say that it really doesn't matter where you start, it is where you finish that counts, I am speaking from personal experience.

DIRECT SELLING—TODAY'S CHOICE!

Direct selling has become the preferred marketing choice of today. Why? Because it is the most efficient way to meet the needs of today's consumers. In our fast-paced world of constantly changing technology and increased knowledge our customers need readily available expert advice to help them weed through the myriad of products and services available. Mass media advertising meets consumers' needs for product information, but, as we are inundated with more and more choices, we are becoming increasingly skeptical and confused by advertising. Department stores are steadily becoming impersonal and, with their constant reduction in staff, less desirable places to shop.

Consumers are busy people, with ever-increasing demands on their time as they raise families, pursue careers, and strive to better themselves physically and intellectually. Many North American families can no longer afford the luxury of one spouse remaining at home. The result is a demand for numerous products and services coupled with a lack of time to learn about and locate the goods an active family needs.

Another important factor in the tremendous success of direct selling is that most products marketed directly are backed by a company guarantee of total client satisfaction. Clients have the right to exchange products or have their full purchase price refunded should they not be satisfied with their purchase. Therefore, direct sales companies must market superior products or they will break the bank honoring their guarantee. The end result is that people have come to trust products sold through direct sales.

It is easy to understand why consumers are turning to direct sales people for the products and services they need. It is also easy to see why so many women and men are choosing direct sales businesses as a full-time or additional source of income. Direct marketing businesses provide unlimited opportunity and very little risk.

Direct sales businesses operate on a dual marketing system. The parent company provides the wholesale product, advertising, training, and support; and the independent consultant retails directly to the consumer. With very little or no risk, consultants enjoy all of the benefits of owning their own business—unlimited income, control over their hours and place of work, tax deductions, and prestige—without the financial and emotional burdens of a totally independent business. Because everyone entering into direct sales learns from the experiences of others, the room for error is minimal. In fact, as long as you are willing to learn and adopt the proven methods outlined in your company manuals and training sessions, and are willing to work consistently at furthering your business and skill levels, you are guaranteed to build a profitable business!

WHAT IS DIRECT MARKETING?

Quite simply, direct marketing refers to taking goods and services directly to the consumer.   More importantly, though, to the independent consultant, direct marketing is the art of matching your clients' needs with your products and services. I refer to marketing as an art because successfully meeting your clients' needs requires tremendous skill on your part. Simply having a great product will not guarantee a suitable match between your goods and your clients. You must be able to determine each of your clients' unique requirements so as to be able to relay how your products and services can fulfill their needs.

Understanding your target market will help you to match effectively your goods and services with clients who will genuinely benefit from using them. What group or type of person needs your products and services? Once you realize who your target market is, matching your clients with your products and services becomes much simpler.

I smile when I think of the number of times I have heard one of our Camelion consultants complain that they tried to sell hosiery to someone who didn't buy because she doesn't wear pantyhose or knee-highs. In Camelion, it is an exception when we do not sell at least one pair of hosiery to a potential client, so I understand that our consultants are taken aback when someone doesn't buy. However, when I hear this complaint I can't help but ask, "Why would you want to sell hosiery to someone who doesn't wear hosiery? There are women everywhere who do wear hosiery; why worry about the few who don't?" No matter what you are marketing, there are people who will buy from you. Never, never get discouraged when someone does not have a need for your product.

Once you have targeted your market, your task is to let your potential clients know that you can help meet their needs. This is where your marketing skills come into play. To be effective you must know your products and be able to project your belief in your products professionally and enthusiastically, communicate effectively with your clients, and cement your client-to-product match with a confident close. We will explore marketing techniques in greater detail later.

THE ROLE OF THE DIRECT SALES PERSON

The first thing I teach new Camelion consultants is that they are not salespeople, but more importantly, they are business people! When you merely sell a product, and not your continuing service, you are in sales. When you sell a product while keeping your clients' needs foremost in importance and with the intention of building a steady clientele, you are truly in business.

A profitable lesson to learn early in your career is the value of repeat business. The initial sale always requires the most effort and education. I say education because effective consultants educate their clients as to how their products and services can best meet their clients' needs. In other words, a direct sales/business person is a teacher and educator.

To be a competent teacher, you must be thoroughly familiar with your products and services. You must also be an attentive listener so that you can discover the individual needs of each of your clients. Of course, you must also have a professional presentation and close. Therefore, the role of the direct sales person is to be the very best teacher and business person possible.

PERFECT PRACTICE MAKES PERFECT!

Practice does not make perfect, perfect practice makes perfect! No matter how much you repeat a task, if you are not doing the task correctly, you will never attain your desired results.

Throughout my career I have witnessed many people continually miss sales and bookings because they refused to use the recommended business techniques. I am particularly sensitive to this problem, because for the first few weeks of my career, I refused to use the "tried and true" methods outlined in the company sales manual. I didn't think the examples for overcoming objections, closing a sale, or booking group demonstrations sounded like me. I insisted on doing things "my way" until, frustrated by poor results, I consulted my manager. For the umpteenth time she suggested I use the company's recommended methods. As usual, I responded with, "I can't use those techniques; they don't sound like me." My manager finally had the courage and wisdom to tell me, "What does sound like you, Joy, doesn't work!" I got the message and I began trying the methods suggested. My sales and bookings improved immediately and continued to grow as my knowledge increased.

Throughout this book and your company sales manual, there are numerous ideas and techniques for building a very profitable direct sales business. Whether you are new to direct sales, or are seeking ways to improve an established business, adopt the methods of the experts. The information in this book alone is the combined knowledge of dozens of successful business people. Don't try to rewrite the manual; instead, practice what you are learning until you can use the techniques confidently and competently.

SET YOUR SIGHTS ON THE SKY!

The only limits in life are the ones you set yourself! Regardless of what you have tried before, or what you have been told or believed you could or couldn't do, you are in total control of your future accomplishments.

Earlier I stated that it does not matter where you start, instead, it is where you finish that counts. For years I believed I was stupid. I believed I was dim-witted so deeply that I refused to study for exams throughout my grade school years. Thank goodness I was not nearly as dumb as I thought I was and in spite of my low self-esteem and ambition, I passed each grade. It wasn't until I decided to compete with a girl friend in sixth grade that I began to discover my academic abilities. In seventh grade I actually achieved the second highest standing in my class. Still, I was not totally convinced that I could do well academically and my grades began to slip again until I finally quit school in tenth grade.

Fortunately my mother made me promise to finish twelfth grade at night school. A promise is a promise, and two years later I returned to college to complete my education. Afraid I would fail, I studied diligently. You guessed it! My grades were always A's and B's. I started to realize that perhaps I wasn't dumb; however, it wasn't until I went to college that I truly began to believe I was intelligent. I had learned an important lesson. If you are willing to keep trying, learning, and growing, you will eventually possess the knowledge, confidence, and ability to succeed. Becoming successful requires that you never give up on yourself and that you never fall victim to your own or others' doubts about you!

Whenever I think of the limits we place on ourselves, or the limits we allow others to place on us, I am reminded of a story about a radio broadcaster who could not read. For years this fellow had the afternoon show on a local radio station. One day it was discovered that he was illiterate and he was fired. Lacking formal education, he decided to open a corner automobile servicing station. Within a few years he opened his second, then third and fourth gas station. By the time he retired, he owned a large chain of service stations and had become a millionaire. At his retirement party a well-meaning friend made the comment, "Just imagine how well you would have done if you could read." "Yes," came the millionaire's response, "I would still be a radio broadcaster!"

I love this story because it reinforces the fact that we, not others or circumstances, limit ourselves. It also serves as a reminder that when life serves you lemons, a way exists to turn your misfortune into lemonade. Remember, never, never limit yourself through a lack of belief in what you can do!

WHY WOMEN IN PARTICULAR EXCEL IN SALES!

It is a fact that women are becoming increasingly successful in sales, management, and business. Many bosses who previously excluded females from marketing and management are now seeking women to fill these same positions. Why? Because, as a gender we are proving our capabilities over and over again. Women are not quitters. Since we were children we have been raised to stick with tasks and people until the end. We are taught to be nurturers and listeners.

Listening, the act of hearing and responding, is a key component in many aspects of business. Combined with nurturing, our listening skills become extremely powerful. Now, add determination to your list—a refusal to give up because you did not succeed at first—and you have an effective formula for success! It is no wonder that women are succeeding, when in addition to these skills, like men, we are also intelligent, patient, and goal oriented.

ARE YOU WILLING TO BE YOUR BEST?

I ask the question, "Are you willing to be your best?" to re-emphasize that your commitment to your business *will* determine your success. No single factor will affect your business more! For years I remember thinking of myself as a racehorse confined within a stall. I wanted to run with life, yet, I held myself back. I had a million excuses for not achieving all that I was capable of: I'm too tired to do more; my family needs me; I'm already doing more than most people; I'm still young, I will accomplish more later. Yet, I wasn't quite satisfied with the way my life was unfolding.

One day I decided to see just how much I could accomplish if I truly committed to fulfilling all of my dreams. Wow, what a difference an attitude makes! I have discovered that I can run a direct marketing company, write a book, speak publicly, and still have enough energy to socialize. Accomplishing more is simply a matter of believing in yourself and doing more. Yes, sometimes I get tired and must rest. Occasionally I wonder if I will ever accomplish all I have set out to do. Still, I keep working toward my goals. Why? Because I am committed to being the best I can be!

Varying reasons hold different people back. Releasing your inner power requires an understanding of where you want to go (your goals) and what is holding you back (your inhibitions). Goals and inhibitions are powerful forces guiding your future achievements.

Without goals you do not have a clearly defined forward direction and will drift endlessly. You will never arrive at your destination because you do not have a destination. In other words, you will not put all of your energy into play without knowing where you are going, as well as when and how you are going to get there. Goals are as fundamental to success as a foundation is to a house!

Unfortunately, inhibitions and fears paralyze numerous competent people. As silly as it sounds, many people fear success while others fear failure. Some individuals fear ridicule and rejection; others fear change. A multitude of people fear loss...loss of respect, reputation, security, health, friends, or family.

Because they seldom come true, fears are the saddest reasons I know for not going after exactly what you want. In reality, F.E.A.R. is merely an acronym for False Expectations Appearing Real. That is not to say there is never any danger in changing your life patterns or income source...there is. But, with the right attitude, clearly defined goals, and a well-developed plan, you can accomplish even your wildest dream!

WHAT IF YOU DO FAIL?

Abandoning your fears and taking risks does not mean forsaking common sense. However, in order to facilitate personal and professional growth, you must be willing to risk. Although the possibility of failure is inherent in every risk you take, success is equally probable. In fact, confidence, courage, and success are developed one risk at a time! Only by taking chances can you succeed. When you succeed, you become more confident and courageous. It is also a fact that failure is a powerful developmental tool. Provided you learn from your mistakes and do not stop risking, failure can actually help you to develop the expertise required to achieve your goals.

During my business career, it is the things that I have failed at from which I have learned the most. If you doubt this, stop and think of how many times an organization will change something that is working well, to try something new, only to find that it was getting better results from its original methods. In Camelion, I once made the decision to do away with our starter kits for new consultants. Why? Because our managers had convinced me that many new consultants couldn't afford their starter kits. The argument was that new consultants would begin with a manual and hosiery color swatch, then, as they began to make money, they could purchase their training tapes, flip chart, etc.

What we discovered was that new consultants couldn't possibly succeed without their training material and they were quitting their Camelion businesses before they got them off the ground. Within six months we had reinstated our policy that new consultants must purchase starter kits. Of course, our managers have convinced me to make many positive changes in Camelion. And, thank goodness, most of our changes are positive. My point is simply that failure produces learning and should be respected, not feared.

Hopefully you already possess an understanding of what you would like to achieve and what is holding you back. However, don't worry if you are not aware of your goals and/or inhibitions, as we will study both in the chapter on goal setting. Right now I would like you to start believing in your ability to do anything you commit to doing, and commit to being your best!

WHAT DOES BUILDING A BUSINESS REALLY MEAN?

Instant fame and fortune is what winning the lottery is about, not what building a business is about. Some individuals enter direct sales believing they will immediately succeed at every aspect of their business and start with an income in the six digit bracket! Wanting instantaneous success is fine, provided it does not prevent you from continuing with your business when you experience your first setback.

A direct sales business can lead to a six digit income, but first it must be built! Building a business means establishing a loyal clientele of repeat customers. This takes time, dedication, and work!

In direct sales, the best place to begin building your business is by building your skill level. We've already talked about learning from the experts in your company and through self-help books. Everywhere you turn in direct sales, people are willing to guide you. Fellow consultants share business secrets and tips, for free! Weekly success meetings are brain-storming sessions for higher and higher profits. There are sales training audio and video cassettes. In most major cities, there are motivational and self-help seminars offered every month. And, of course, we can learn from our customers.

Early in your career, it is important that you learn to analyze each sale you make, and more importantly, each sale you do not make. Rather than getting upset when you do not sell as much as you wanted to, or when you do not make a sale at all, make a habit of learning from these minor setbacks. When someone doesn't buy, ask yourself why. First, did your prospect have a need for your product or service? If the answer is no, then take a second look at your target clientele. Was your presentation professional and client-centered or were you nervous or disinterested? Be honest; this is your classroom and both you and your future clients stand to benefit from your analysis. Did you close the sale with confidence or did you hesitate? How could you improve next time? Do you need to gather additional product information? Do you need to develop further your style or presentation? Remember, the answers to the above questions are the keys to your future success; therefore, welcome the chance to grow personally and professionally when you do not make the sale you intended.

Once you have fine tuned your business skills, building your business is simply a matter of continually adding to your client base and reservicing your established clientele. Direct selling really is quite simple.

DIRECT SELLING IS SIMPLE, NOT EASY!

Although you may initially find your new direct sales business challenging or overwhelming, do not despair. The skills you are learning will very quickly become second nature. Undoubtedly, you can remember other tasks which you have mastered, yet once found intimidating. Driving an automobile would be a great example. Today, you likely get behind the wheel without thinking about all of the things you will have to concentrate on once you are on the road. If you think back, driving was not always that simple. The first time you took control of a motor vehicle, my bet is that you were terrified. You probably had sweaty palms and a nervous stomach. Most likely you spent five to fifteen minutes positioning the seat so that your feet reached the pedals exactly, and another three to ten minutes adjusting the rear- and side-view mirrors. You probably spent an additional five or more minutes taking deep breaths before you finally started the engine. Once in gear, you likely looked both ways a dozen times before you pulled onto the road. Glancing from the speedometer, to the road signs, to the road probably seemed to take a minute and a half, not the true couple of seconds it actually took. Once back home, you probably kissed the ground and thanked your lucky stars that you and your brave copilot were still intact and breathing. Well, mastering direct sales is a lot easier than learning how to drive a car!

No one has ever lost a life, or even bent a fender, practicing her direct sales skills. And remember, it will not be long until everything you are learning seems like child's play. Once your skills are polished, your business will actually become quite repetitious, yet it will never become boring. Why? Because unlike a stationary office job, you will continually be meeting new and exciting people. Throughout your career, you will meet other business people, doctors, lawyers, university professors, secretaries, homemakers, professional entertainers, waitresses, truck drivers, politicians, and more. Direct selling is fun and very rewarding financially and personally!

EARN WHILE YOU LEARN

One of the most exciting aspects of direct marketing is that while you are learning, you are also earning. Although you may not initially possess all of the skills necessary for long-term success, sheer enthusiasm will ensure you numerous bookings and sales. People love to be around happy individuals and will want to share in the excitement of your new business. Therefore, you can start building your business today!

CONSISTENCY IS THE KEY TO SUCCESS

Like everything that is worthwhile in life, building a direct sales business requires consistent effort and dedication. To be successful you must continually locate new clients as well as service your growing clientele. However, you are in total control of your business and can put as much time into it as you deem will add quality to your life.

Many direct sales people can only devote one night or afternoon a week to their businesses. Other consultants work their businesses full-time. How much time you dedicate to your business is up to you. The most important factor is that you work your business consistently. Realize that, even by conducting one group showing a week with an average of six guests in attendance, over a fifty-week period you will have established 300 clients. Multiply your efforts over five years and you have a client base of 1,500! With regular servicing, 300 or more clients will result in substantial reorder profits.

COPING WITH SKEPTICISM

Unfortunately, whenever you embark on a new venture in life there are always people who are willing to tell you why you will not succeed. Naturally, the action you need to take when confronted by a Doubting Dorothy will vary according to your relationship and degree of involvement with the person.

When the Doubting Dorothy is someone you love, obviously you will want to handle this person with care, especially if it is your mother, husband, sibling, or a close friend. When dealing with Doubting Dorothys, I find that simply listening to their concerns can effectively diminish their fears. In other words, uncovering why they are frightened for you, or for themselves, and reassuring them can be quite healing. It is extremely important, though, that you do not allow their judgment to color yours. If your efforts to reassure a Doubting Dorothy are unsuccessful and you are still receiving a lot of opposition, then perhaps the most you can insist upon is your right to discover your own abilities. Everyone is entitled to choose the challenges in their lives!

Sometimes the Doubting Dorothy in your life is an acquaintance or coworker. In this case, you must decide if your relationship is worth building. It is my opinion that when someone who is not an integral part of your life is consistently negative, it is inadvisable to inform her of your dreams and ambitions. If you find that a particular person totally defeats your energy, perhaps you do not want to spend any time with her. Regardless, never waste precious energy trying to convince others you will succeed. You may never convince them anyway, and will probably end up frustrating yourself.

About three months after Camelion opened, my father asked me how things were going. Well, as in any new business, I had experienced numerous ups and downs, yet I was very optimistic that Camelion would succeed. I responded with, "Business is great, Dad!"

Dad's overprotective probing continued, "No, dear. Tell me the truth. I'm your father. You can be honest with me." We bantered back and forth about three times before I finally had the courage to tell him that his need to protect me was hurting me.

"Dad, if business wasn't going well, what I would need you to say is that I shouldn't worry because if anyone could make Camelion work, I could. And, when I tell you business is doing well, what I need you to say is that you knew I could do it!" My intention, of course, was not to stop my father from caring for me. Rather, I wanted him to understand that he could better care for me by encouraging me to stretch...to be the best that I could be.

My father is quite the character, and he loves to tease. From that day forward, whenever I see Dad he winks and says, "So dear, how is business really going?" Teasing has become Dad's way of reassuring himself that I am doing fine, while continuing to give me support.

Your goals and ambitions are a very private and personal matter. Whom you choose to share them with is up to you. You do not have to answer to anyone but yourself, and no one can affect your business unless you permit her to. Regardless of whether you have the support of others, know in your heart that, provided you are committed, you can and will attain your goals.

FINDING A SUPPORT PERSON

When the person you most want to support you won't, seek support from another source. You will enjoy the pursuit of your goals more when you share them with someone special; however, your business support person does not have to be the closest person to you. It can be a co-worker, a sibling, a parent, your spouse, a fellow consultant, or a friend. Your support person should be someone who truly believes in your goals and your ability to achieve them.

When you select a support person, let that person know you have chosen her and why. Then, ask if she would like to be your support person. When she accepts, tell her how she can help you.

In Camelion, we teach a consultant to work with her support person to compile a list of all of her positive attributes and accomplishments. For instance: I am a good dresser, I am nice, I am intelligent, I am self-motivated, I am a good mother, I am a caring friend, I have nice hair, I am a great cook, I am very loving, I have neat handwriting, I am a great speller, I am fun to be with, I am a great salesperson. Both you and your support person should keep a copy of your list. Then, whenever you are feeling a little down, you both have a ready reference as to why you should start feeling good about yourself again.

Your support person should be the person you turn to whenever you are feeling discouraged or overwhelmed. Her role is simply to reinforce your goals and abilities to achieve what you desire. A true support person wants you to succeed and will enjoy each step you take on your way to the top!

YOUR DIARY TO SUCCESS

At the end of each chapter you will find a brief summary of what we have learned, followed by a diary to success. Your diary to success is designed for you to keep notes on the points you feel are most pertinent to your business and your success. Also use your diary to list things you would like to accomplish, areas where you need to improve, and promises you are making to yourself.

CHAPTER SUMMARY

• In direct selling, it does not matter where you start; it is where you finish that counts.

• Direct selling has become today's preferred marketing choice because it is the most efficient way to meet the needs of today's consumers.

• The role of the direct sales person is to be the very best teacher and business person possible.

• The only limits in life are the ones you set for yourself.

• Commitment to your business goals is paramount to your success.

• In order to facilitate personal and professional growth you must be willing to take risks; however, abandoning your fears and taking risks does not mean forsaking common sense.

• Building a business means establishing a loyal clientele of repeat customers. This takes time, dedication, and work.

• Although you may initially find your new direct sales business challenging and overwhelming, do not despair. The skills you are learning will very quickly become second nature.

• One of the most exciting aspects of direct marketing is that while you are learning, you are also earning.

• Regardless of whether you have the support of others, know in your heart that, provided you are committed, you can and will attain your goals.

DIARY TO SUCCESS

CHAPTER TWO

Prospecting for Clients

As a direct sales person, you are most likely marketing a product which is used in numerous households or businesses in North America. As such, you are never without potential clients! The key to success, however, is knowing how to reach effectively your prospective clients.

LOCATING CLIENTS WHEN YOU ARE NEW

When you are new, the best place to begin your business is with your friends, acquaintances, coworkers, and family. It is a fact that most people know approximately two hundred people. Of course, you are not in constant contact with everyone you know. Perhaps you have not even spoken or written to some of your acquaintances for many years. Nevertheless, you do know enough people to build a foundation for your business.

Starting your business through friends does not mean that you should rely on them for a constant source of sales. Your friends are only the beginning of a varied and far-reaching client base.

There are two reasons why you should begin your business with the people you know. The first is that your friends, relatives, and coworkers are the people with whom you likely feel the most comfortable. Many business consultants are a little nervous when they conduct their first business appointments, or group demonstrations, so the more comfort you can attain at this time, the better you will feel.

Unlike strangers, many of your friends and family want you to succeed and will happily book group showings and individual appointments to see the products you are so excited about marketing. Later, when you are more experienced and confident, booking with strangers will become equally easy. In the beginning, though, your enthusiasm is your most effective booking tool and will compensate for any skills you lack.

You should never feel guilty about presenting your friends with an opportunity to own and benefit from the superior products or services you market. (If you do not feel your products or services are superior, you should not be marketing them to anyone!) You are not using your friends when you offer them goods they need, that are first-rate, and that they would buy from another source if they weren't dealing with you…someone they care about and who they know cares about them!

Even though booking with people you know is relatively easy, before you call even your closest friend to arrange a showing, *read Chapter 3 on booking!* The earlier you begin practicing and perfecting your booking techniques, the sooner you will be able to service and help more people. If you start asking for bookings before you have studied the techniques, you may not get the results you want and become disheartened. Once you are familiar with how to book, however, you will easily make appointments with friends and strangers.

WHAT IF SOMEONE I CARE ABOUT DOES NOT WANT TO BOOK?

Inevitably, someone you thought was going to be excited about your new business and products isn't interested at all. More so than strangers, a discouraging friend can crush your enthusiasm. Earlier we talked about some of the reasons why people might not immediately support your new business venture; yet, regardless of the rationale behind a friend's disapproval, it still hurts.

The best thing to do when a friend demonstrates disinterest in your business is to drop the subject and, from that point forward, avoid talking about your business with that particular person. Eventually, your friend will likely enquire as to how your business is doing. When she does, satisfy her curiosity with a brief statement, then change the subject. Later, should your friend ask to view your product line, professionally arrange an appointment.

The reason I suggest the above approach is that it is futile to try and convince others to support your business. Supporting you is a choice they must make for themselves. Trying to get someone excited for you will only lead to you feeling rejected and hurt, so don't bother.

I remember a story told to me by one of our Camelion managers. Her daughter, a dental assistant, was wearing Camelion hosiery and was bragging to a fellow worker about how wonderful it was. Her coworker responded by stating that she had been buying the same brand of hosiery for years and was not interested in trying Camelion. The manager's daughter was hurt, but shrugged off the incident, never again bringing up the subject. Well you guessed it! Two years later, her coworker decided she did want to purchase Camelion non-run hosiery. The evening before she had ruined two pairs of pantyhose before she had left the house for an outing with her husband. The two pairs of hosiery had cost her over seven dollars. Suddenly it dawned on the coworker that she should stop wasting her money on hosiery that ran. So you see, if you don't try to convince people that you are right, they may eventually come around on their own, and if they never change their minds, you will not have wasted valuable energy.

PROSPECTING FOR CLIENTS USING DOUBLE BUSINESS CARDS

Double business cards are perforated in the center. One half of the card displays your name, address, phone number, and business logo. The other half provides a place for you to record the name, address, and phone number of a potential client.

Sample Double Business Card

CAMELION
Susan Hargis
Independent Fashion Accessory Consultant
555 5th Avenue South
Phoenix, Arizona
00000
Phone: (602) 555-5555

— — — — — — — — - Perforated Line · — — — — — — — — —

Prospect's Name: _____

Address: _____

Phone Number: _____

In bank lines, waiting for a bus, through friends and work you meet new people every day. These individuals are prospective clients. "What do you do for a living?" is a common inquiry made by new acquaintances. This question provides a great opening for you to introduce your product line by saying, "Well, what I am most excited about is my business!" Your new acquaintance will likely ask what you are marketing, paving the way for you to: talk about your products or business opportunity, offer her your business card, and ask for her name and phone number. Study the following sample to see the natural flow of turning casual meetings into business leads.

SAMPLE CONVERSATION
FOR TURNING CASUAL ACQUAINTANCES
INTO BUSINESS PROSPECTS

Prospect: "What do you do for a living?" or "What is new and exciting in your life?"

Your response: "Actually, I've just started a new business."

Prospect: "Really! What is your new business?"

Your response: "I'm an independent consultant with Every Person's Marketing Choice. What I am most excited about is that our members can purchase numerous products at discount and wholesale prices. I couldn't believe it when I first learned how much money I could save by joining our organization. Our products are excellent, and whether or not you are a member, Every Person's Marketing Choice offers you shopping variety and savings! (Pause.) Let me give you my card. (Take out your business card, tear the card apart and hand your prospect the portion with your name and phone number. Keep the second half of the card in your hand and take out your pen.)

Note: Remember, you want to look professional, so keep your double business cards and a pen in an easily accessible place.

Prospect: "I've heard of Every Person's Marketing Choice."

Your response: "I'm sure you have heard of us. We've been around for years. Actually, what I should do is give you a call and tell you about our newest product additions. I know you'll be impressed. (Then, without hesitating for a second, ask for her home phone number.) What is your number at home?"

Provided that you conduct the above conversation confidently and comfortably, your prospective client should give you her home phone number.

TIPS FOR FOLLOWING UP WITH PROSPECTS

Following up with a prospective client to book an appointment is quite easily accomplished, provided you follow a few simple rules. When you call your prospect, always:

1) State who you are and how you met. ("Hello, Anna. This is Gabriela Estevez. I am the Every Person's Marketing Choice distributor you met at Tom and Sue's party on the weekend. How are you?")

2) State why you are calling and make a point of using the word "promise" in your opening remarks. ("I promised I would call you and tell you about our latest products.") The benefit of using the word "promise" is that your prospect will feel that if you are keeping your promise to call, then she should keep her implied promise to listen to you. Once she is listening, booking the appointment becomes easy!

3) Ask if this is a convenient time for your potential client to talk. ("Anna, I know you are a busy lady so I won't take up too much of your time. Before I start though, is this a convenient time for you to talk with me?") If your potential client says she cannot talk right then, simply ask when would be a better time for you to call back. If she says that she has a few minutes, then continue.

4) In a professional and enthusiastic manner, briefly tell your prospect about your products or business opportunity. ("Anna, as you know, Every Person's Marketing Choice has a superior line of household cleaning products, vitamins, and skin care. I truly believe every consumer has a right to enjoy the quality and savings that using our products provides. However, I also believe everyone should purchase their goods at wholesale prices, and I want to offer you the opportunity to do just that! Are you aware that when you become a distributor with our company, you can now purchase everything from television sets to cars at discounted and wholesale prices?")

5) Confidently, ask for the booking. ("Anna, we really must get together so that I can explain everything to you in detail. I want you to discover how you will benefit from using our products and our business opportunity. Is there any reason why we couldn't get together one day this week?")

Note: When booking you must be confident at all times. Hesitate, and your booking will be lost. Avoid weak phrases such as: "Do you think…?" "Would it be possible…?" "Could we get together…?" "Are you interested…?" These types of phrases lead to excuses from your potential clients as to why they can't meet with you. Study the chapter on booking appointments for more information on confident booking strategies and closes.

COLD CALLING USING DOUBLE BUSINESS CARDS

Whether you market cosmetics, hosiery, clothing, jewelry, household items, water filters, color analyses, encyclopedias, insurance, cars, lingerie, beer kits, three-dimensional cameras, or diet and health aids…everyone you meet is a prospective client. A prospective client is anyone who may need your services or products for herself or someone she cares about. Cold calling using double business cards is an effective way for you to turn strangers into clients.

When I started my full-time career in Mary Kay Cosmetics, I had just moved to Vancouver, British Columbia. As I only knew a handful of people, I needed a much larger client base. A friend and fellow Mary Kay consultant volunteered to teach me how to cold call. The idea of offering a complete stranger a complimentary facial was extremely intimidating for me. I was certain I would die from fright. My friend reassured me that I would survive, told me what to say, and off I went to the shopping mall. I am certain that the reason the first woman I approached gave me her name and phone number was that she felt sorry for me. Instead of presenting myself confidently and professionally, I stuttered and blushed. In fact, I was shaking so violently that when she gave me her name and phone number, I couldn't connect my pen with my business card. Thank goodness, the woman volunteered to write down the information for me.

Afterward I was ecstatic! I had a prospective client! I knew that if I could survive cold calling once, I could do it again and again. And, with a never ending source of clients, I would have a successful business.

Since that first day, I learned that the more confident you are, the more names and phone numbers you will obtain. Following are guidelines for successful cold calling with strangers.

1) Wear a business outfit. You want to look professional when prospecting for clients.

2) Don't carry a briefcase. Consumers have been programmed to say no to salespeople before they have even heard what is being offered. You want your potential clients to see you as a person first, and a busi-

ness person second.

3) Keep your business cards and a pen readily available.

4) Approach people who look friendly, and who you believe would benefit from knowing about your products and services.

5) Be prepared! Write out your approach and practice it until you are certain you will remember your script even when you are nervous. Rehearsing in front of a mirror will allow you to watch your facial expressions.

6) Keep your cold calling presentation informative, upbeat, and short. People walking down the street, shopping in a mall, or waiting for a bus do not have a lot of time to talk.

7) Plan your cold calling periods for when people are out and about. I find that I obtain the most leads between eleven in the morning and two in the afternoon.

8) As prospective clients may be nervous about giving you their last name, only ask for their first. And, as some individuals will prefer to give you their work number, ask for their number at home or at work. The less threatening you are, the more leads you will acquire.

9) If you are nervous, ask a fellow consultant to accompany you.

10) Take your sense of humor and adventure along with you! Some people will tell you that they are not interested in hearing what you have to say, so you will have to accept a little rejection. Don't worry though. They are not rejecting you, they are simply dismissing the idea of trusting a stranger or perhaps spending money. Regardless, a little rejection will not hurt you.

11) If you receive two or three rejections in a row, recharge your energy with a cup of coffee and your favorite motivational book. Then tackle your task again. Going home is for the weakhearted...not the adventuresome.

12) Get excited. In fact, get ecstatic! People want to be around happy, enthusiastic people.

13) As you approach a prospective client, smile and look directly into her eyes. Chances are she will relax and return your smile.

14) Make a habit of cold calling one or two people per day and you will never be without clients. In fact, your business will build very rapidly!

SAMPLE COLD CALLING APPROACH

Your opening line: "Excuse me, my name is Diane Stone. I am a consultant with Looking Good Cosmetics. Have you heard of us? We have a remarkable skin care and makeup line." (Take out your business card, tear it in half, and give your prospective client the portion with your name and phone number. Hold the second half of the card in your hand and reach for your pen.)

Prospect: "No, I don't think I have."

Your response: "Well, today is your lucky day because I am going to offer you a complimentary consultation. Our product line is quite unique in that all of our products are hypo-allergenic."

Prospect: "Hypo-allergenic...that's good."

Your response: "Yes, it is good. I think you will also be impressed by the fact that all of our eye shadows, base makeup, and blushers are categorized into the four different skin tone groups. Have you ever been color analyzed?"

Prospect: "No I haven't, but I would like to be."

Your response: "I would be pleased to color analyze you and I realize that you probably do not have a lot of time to chat right now. What I would like to do is take your first name and your phone number at home or work, so that I can give you a quick call and tell you a bit more." (Pose with your pen ready to write on the remaining half of your double business card.)

Note: The phrase "What I would like to do is..." is a soft yet powerful request that generally elicits a positive response. Remember, a statement such as, "Could I please have your phone number?", is weak and will lead to rejection. When you make confident statements, prospective clients feel you believe in the products you are marketing; equally true, clients interpret weak questions asked by you as evidence that you do not truly believe that your products are superior.

Notice that the above example suggests that you tell your prospect you will give her a "quick" call and "tell her a bit more." This approach is far less threatening than saying you will call them to arrange an appointment. Booking the appointment is your second step and will be accomplished much more easily, later, when you telephone your potential client with additional information.

SAMPLE FOLLOW-UP PHONE CALL

Your follow-up phone call to a prospect you have met through cold calling should be made within two business days of your initial contact. You want to recontact prospects while they are still excited about meeting you and hearing about your products.

Your approach: "Annette. This is Diane Stone. I am the Looking Good Cosmetics consultant you met in the mall yesterday. I promised I would call you and tell you a bit more about our products and services. Before I begin, though, how are you doing and do you have a quick minute to talk?"

Prospect: "I'm fine. But a little busy right now."

Your response: "I'm sorry. Maybe it would be better if I called you at home?"

Prospect: "No, I can talk now as long as you will only take a minute."

Your response: "Great. Well, as I told you the other day, Looking Good Cosmetics are hypo-allergenic. This means that our products do not contain perfume or other ingredients that might irritate your skin. Are you using a skin care program now?"

Prospect: "Yes, I am. I use A.B.C. Cosmetics."

Your response: "Are you completely satisfied with A.B.C. Cosmetics?"

Prospect: "I don't know whether I am completely satisfied, but I have been using A.B.C. for years. I really haven't thought much about it."

Your response: "I understand. Before I discovered Looking Good Cosmetics I had been using another brand of skin care for years. However, when I changed to Looking Good's program, I was amazed at how much healthier my skin looked. Annette, I know you are busy and I promised to keep this call short. Why don't we do this? Why don't we book a time for me to show you what I am talking about? Trying our products is believing and I would love to give you a complimentary skin care and makeup consultation. Is there any reason why we couldn't get together one day this week?"

Prospect: "This is a bad week for me. I am working overtime almost every night."

Your response: "You poor thing. No problem. Which evening next week would be good for you?"

Prospect: "Why don't you give me a call on Monday and I will let you know?"

Your response: "Well I could do that; however, by Monday I may not have any evenings left open next week. Why don't we do this? Why don't we pick a tentative date that we think will work for both of us? If it turns out that we have to change the date, we will. By choosing a tentative date, though, I will at least have an evening reserved for you."

Prospect: "We could do that!"

Your response: "Great. Which is better for you, the beginning of next week or the end of the week?"

Notice in the above example that Diane did not give up when Annette raised the objection that she was too busy to book an appointment. Instead, Diane remained confident, emphasized the value of her own time, and suggested they meet the following week.

PROSPECTING FOR CLIENTS
THROUGH REFERRALS

Asking your clients for the names and phone numbers of people they feel would benefit from knowing about your product line is an effective method for locating future prospects.

Referral systems are most effective when incentives, or gifts, are offered for leads obtained. Incentives can include: discounts on future purchases, complimentary product samples, small prewrapped surprise gifts, or the opportunity to participate in a drawing for a special prize. (The cost of gifts given as incentives should not exceed 5 percent of your expected return.)

Regardless of your incentive, it is important that you remain confident when asking for referrals. Assuring your client that her friends will be pleased to be offered the opportunity to see your products is also important. Study the following sample.

SAMPLE CONVERSATION FOR ASKING
FOR REFERRALS

Your approach: "George, I know you and your wife are going to be extremely pleased with your new bottled water kit. You will save money and have purified water at your fingertips. You know, George, there are many people who have never tasted purified water. I would like to change that. Who do you know that would appreciate using a demonstration filter for a week? Of course, for helping me and your friends, you will automatically be entered in my weekly drawing for two complimentary theatre tickets."

Client: "I don't know if I feel comfortable with the idea of giving you the names of my friends."

Your response: "Don't worry. I am simply going to offer your friends the free use of my water filtering system for one week. You were pleased to be able to use our filter, and your friends will be too. If someone hadn't

given me your name, I could have never helped you and your wife."
   Client: "I suppose you are right. Let me think for a moment."

SOLICITING FOR LEADS BY TELEPHONE

   On days when you must remain in the house or office, the telephone may be your only means of making new contacts.
   Enthusiasm, confidence, and a well-rehearsed approach are essential when cold calling over the phone. You must sound enthusiastic because your prospect is using only one sense, hearing, to make her decision whether to trust you and book with you. Your presentation must be quick, informative, and convincing! In fact, if you hesitate or sound weak, your prospect will simply tell you she is not interested. Let's look at the following sample calls to a business.

SAMPLE #1

   Your approach: "May I please speak with the manager?"
   Receptionist: "Yes. May I ask who is calling?"
   Your response: "Betty Creston." (Just give your name. You do not want the receptionist, or the owner, to screen your call before you have a chance to complete your presentation.)
   Manager: "Hello. Janet Montgomery speaking."
   Your response: "Ms. Montgomery. This is Betty Creston. I am an independent consultant with Classy Clothing Coordinates. Have you heard of us?"
   Manager: "Yes, I have. You sell fashion knit clothing."
   Your response: "That's right. I also teach small groups of employees how to dress professionally, which is the reason I am calling you. My emphasis is on wardrobe coordinating and the fact that you only have one chance to make a first impression! I also cover the importance of good grooming and a professional attitude. I would like to meet with you to discuss the possibility of conducting a presentation for your staff. I know your employees will enjoy the tips I will give them on scarf tying and accessorizing. And, being a business woman, I know you expect your employees to look their best at all times. Is there any reason why we couldn't get together one day this week?"
   Manager: "Everyone here dresses professionally. And, I don't think we have the budget or time for that sort of thing."
   Your response: "Ms. Montgomery, I find that professionally dressed women appreciate and benefit the most from my class. They are already

interested in fashion and are eager to explore new ideas! I realize that your employees' time is valuable, which is why I suggest that the class be held during the lunch hour. Of course, attendance would be on a voluntary basis. There is no charge for my class and I believe you and your staff will be favorably impressed with my presentation!"

Manager: "Fine. Why don't you stop by and see me on Thursday just before noon?"

SAMPLE #2

Your approach: "May I please speak with the receptionist?"

Receptionist: "I am the receptionist."

Your response: "Hello. My name is Carmen Sommerfield. I have a product that I think you and the other women in your office have a right to know about!"

Receptionist: "What product do you have?"

Your response: "I have exotic perfume replicas from around the world including Oscar de la Renta, Joy, and Giorgio! Our beautiful fragrances are today's woman's answer to affordable luxury. I know you will love them and I would like to drop by and give you a complimentary sample of your favorite scent. I would also like your opinion on whether you feel the other women in your office would appreciate an opportunity to try their favorite scents."

Receptionist: "Canvassing is prohibited in our office and I am too busy to meet with you."

Your response: "Don't worry. I will place your complimentary sample in an envelope with your name on it and quickly drop it off at your desk."

Receptionist: "Okay. My name is Ann Day."

Your response: "Great, Ann! I will drop your free sample off one day this week."

Of course, distributing free product samples, or catalogs, to receptionists in your area is a great idea, even if you do not start with a phone call. The advantage of phoning first is that you will have the receptionist's name and attention beforehand.

PROSPECTING THROUGH DISTRIBUTING
CATALOGS OR FREE PRODUCT SAMPLES

Distributing free product samples, or catalogs, is a great way to meet prospective clients; however, there is a second vital step. Simply leaving a sample or a brochure will not lead to a sale. You must follow up with your prospective clients by phone or in person. Therefore, whenever you give away a complimentary sample, remember to ask for the recipient's name and phone number.

Your approach: "Good morning. My name is Marie Paget and I have a gift for you. It is a catalog of Your Life Health Care Aids. Our vitamins and diet aids are recommended by numerous naturopath practitioners across the country. All of our products are derived from organically grown vegetation and are easily absorbed by your body. Of course, our products are backed by a company guarantee of total client satisfaction. Have you heard of Your Life Health Care Aids?"

Receptionist: "Yes I have."

Your response: "Great! Then you know about the fantastic results people get from using our products. Are you on a vitamin program now?"

Receptionist: "I take vitamins every day but I don't know if you would call it a vitamin program."

Your response: "I would be pleased to help you develop a complete vitamin program, but I don't want to take any more of your time right now. Why don't I give you a call at home and we can discuss what vitamins you are currently taking to make certain you are getting the correct amounts and varieties? In the meantime, if you have a free moment, take a look at our catalog. What is your first name?"

Receptionist: "Jeannette."

Your response: "Jeannette, what is your phone number at home?"

Note: The principles for following up leads obtained while distributing product samples or catalogs are the same as those outlined under cold calling using double business cards.

DOOR-TO-DOOR SOLICITING

Avon and Fuller Brush have been marketing their products door-to-door for years. Although many women are now working outside the home, there are still numerous people home during the week. Of course, even more people are home on Saturday.

The biggest advantage of marketing products door-to-door is that you can complete your prospecting call and demonstration in one step.

There are two things that you must be prepared for when you solicit customers in their home. The first is that you will have to knock on from three to five doors before you will locate someone at home, so be prepared for some good healthy exercise. The second is that you will experience some rejection. People are preprogrammed to say, "I am not interested," even before they hear what you have to offer. Don't worry when this happens to you. Instead, apologize for having disturbed the person, and go on to the next door. Remember, business is a "numbers game" and although some people will not be interested, many prospects will become happy clients.

When a prospect opens her door, make a point of smiling and extending your hand in a gesture to shake hers. Your prospect will likely smile and shake your hand. However, if she does not, remain composed and quickly state who you are and why you knocked on her door.

SAMPLE DOOR-TO-DOOR
CANVASSING CONVERSATION

Your approach: "Good afternoon. (Big smile. Extend your hand in a gesture to shake his.) My name is Chad O'Neill and I would like to show you our revolutionary new three-dimensional camera. Without a doubt, ours is the most fascinating camera of today. Are you the photographer in the family?"

Prospect: "No, my wife is. I am a terrible photographer."

Your response: "I am certain, with a little help and the right camera, you would be a great photographer. Let me show you a few pictures I photographed using our three-dimensional camera. Notice how my subject stands out while the background recedes. I love the effect of the cherry blossoms in the foreground. I am not a professional photographer and if I can achieve results like this, you can too!"

Prospect: "You think so, do you? How much does your camera cost?"

Your response: "Actually it is quite affordable, but before we go into that what I would like to do is come inside and show you how simple it is to operate."

Prospect: "I am going out in a while."

Your response: "It will only take a couple of minutes. I promise."

Prospect: "Okay. Come in."

Once inside your prospect's home, you can easily complete your presentation and close the sale.

PROSPECTING FOR CLIENTS
THROUGH NETWORKING

Networking is one of the easiest and most effective ways of locating clients, yet very few business people take advantage of this steady source of prospects.

Networking is the active pursuit of clients through interaction with other business people. The philosophy of networking is, "I will scratch your back if you scratch mine." In other words, I will refer clients to you if you do the same for me.

Many clubs and organizations will allow you to attend their meetings as a guest, so you can network without joining a particular affiliation. Make a habit of exchanging business cards with people you meet through organizations such as business clubs, women's groups, and motivational seminars.

Exchanging client lists with another direct sales person can be equally beneficial. If you are both retailing products with a common target market, and your products are not competitive, why not exchange names and promote one another?

Following are guidelines for networking.

1) Only share your clients' names with reputable business people marketing superior products.

2) Never give a client's name out to more than one other business person.

3) Where possible, inform your client that you plan to give, or have already given, her name and phone number to another business person.

PRODUCT SATISFACTION SURVEYS

Information gathered through surveying the hosiery needs of friends and acquaintances led to the ultimate design of Camelion as a sheer, non-run hosiery, available in many styles, colors and sizes. Today, our consultants still conduct hosiery satisfaction surveys with women who are not Camelion clients. Through these surveys, our consultants continually hear the same complaints that we did when we designed Camelion...expense, availability, and comfort. Once a woman has voiced her complaints about the hosiery she is currently wearing, she is intrigued by the fact that Camelion hosiery is designed to alleviate all of the problems she has mentioned.

Product satisfaction surveys are an excellent way to meet prospective clients and can be developed and conducted by anyone. The first step is to design a set of questions that will uncover the "needs and wants" of the consumer in relation to the type of product(s) you market. Study the following example.

COLOR ANALYSIS SURVEY

Purpose of survey: To determine the need for color analysis in today's image-conscious society.

1) Have you ever been color analyzed? Yes_____ No_____

2) Do you believe an awareness of which colors best suit your skin tone would help you in selecting future wardrobe pieces? Yes_____ No_____

3) Do you think that knowing which colors suit you best would prevent you from wasting money on clothing and accessories which do not easily mix with your established wardrobe? Yes_____ No_____

4) Would dressing in colors that suit you best make you feel more confident about your personal appearance? Yes_____ No_____

5) Do you think that a color analysis consultation would be a great gift to give to a friend? Yes_____ No_____

6) Do you believe men should be color analyzed? Yes_____ No_____

7) Is a professional image important in your line of work? Yes_____ No_____

Name_____ Phone Number_____

Address_____

_____ Today's Date_____

Product satisfaction surveys can be conducted outside of a mall, on the street, or by telephone. When conducting surveys remember to dress professionally, be confident, and smile!

Notice that in the above sample, the purpose of the survey is stated at the top of the sheet. The purpose of the survey is your opening line when you ask someone to participate.

Product surveys should be short and sweet. The questions asked must be pertinent and easy to answer. As the purpose of your survey is to meet prospective clients, you will want to make certain you obtain everyone's name and phone number.

In the above sample the space for the survey participant's name is at the end of the questionnaire. It is much easier to obtain a participant's name at the end of the survey when you have already established a certain rapport. Study the following examples for obtaining a prospect's name and phone number.

Example #1—to be used if your prospect answered that she has never been color analyzed.

Your approach: "I want to thank you for helping me with my survey and give you one of my business cards. As you can see from the card, my name is Patti-Lee. What is your first name?"

Participant: "Melissa."

Your response: "Thank you for participating in my survey. Melissa, I would like to offer you a complimentary color analysis consultation. I am a trained color and makeup consultant with The Beauty of You Cosmetics. After we have determined your skin tone and season I will demonstrate that wearing the correct eye shadow, blush, base, and lipstick shade is essential for a polished look. Is there any reason why you wouldn't want to be color analyzed?"

Participant: "What is the catch? Why would you give me a free color analysis consultation?"

Your response: "There is no catch. Free color analysis is a service I offer my clients. As I told you, I am also a makeup consultant with The Beauty of You Cosmetics. One of the wonderful features of our line is that our makeup is coded according to each of the four skin tones or seasons. Color analyzing allows me to be certain I am recommending the correct makeup shades for my clients. Melissa, do you agree that knowing your season would be a great advantage when you are shopping for makeup, accessories, and clothes?"

Participant: "I guess you are right."

Your response: "Melissa, I know you do not have a lot of time to talk right now. Why don't I call you at home or at work and answer any other questions that you might have?"

Participant: "I would prefer that you call me at home. My number is 555-5555."

Example #2—to be used if your prospect answered that she has been color analyzed.

Your approach: "I want to thank you for helping me with my survey and give you one of my business cards. As you can see from the card, my name is Patti-Lee. What is your first name?"

Participant: "Rayna."

Your response: "Thank you for participating in my survey, Rayna! You answered that you have been color analyzed before. What season are you?"

Participant: "I'm a winter."

Your response: "Rayna, you can see from my business card that as well as being a color expert, I am a consultant with The Beauty of You Cosmetics. I can tell that you know the importance of wearing the correct makeup shades and I would love to show you our 'winter' color palettes."

Participant: "I don't need any makeup right now."

Your response: "That's fine, Rayna. I still want to show you our 'winter' colors so that the next time you do need makeup you will know that our cosmetics match perfectly with your skin tone and wardrobe. I realize your time is valuable, though, so why don't I take your phone number at home or work and give you a quick call and answer any other questions you might have?"

Participant: "Okay, my number at work is 222-2222."

PROSPECTING THROUGH TRADE FAIRS

Most direct sale companies encourage consultants to participate in local trade fairs. As most people attending fairs are browsing, not buying, concentrate on obtaining leads. Holding a free drawing for a prize will attract people to your display and is an excellent way to meet prospective customers. As people like to enter drawings, the prize you give away does not have to be expensive.

For best results, use a draw form which asks each entrant for their name, address and phone number. The form should also contain questions as to whether the entrant: uses or has ever heard of your products; would be interested in an individual or group demonstration; and, would like to know about your business opportunity.

Within two weeks of the end of the fair, call every entrant, including those who responded negatively to all of the questions on the drawing form. People attending fairs are often rushed and do not read the questions asked on drawing forms; therefore, it is unlikely that they will remember what they answered.

FOLLOWING UP WITH A DRAWING ENTRANT

Your approach: "Hello, is Mary Sundowner there please?"

Entrant: "This is Mary Sundowner."

Your response: "Hello Mary, this is Eunice Ray. I am with Lacy Lady Lingerie. You entered our drawing at the trade fair last week."

Entrant: "Oh. Did I win?"

Your response: "I wish you had. The woman who did win was from your area, though! I'm calling because we promised we would call everyone and tell them a bit more about our Lacy Lady Lingerie line. Is this a convenient time for you to talk?"

Entrant: "Yes, I have a couple of minutes."

Your response: "It will just take a minute. You indicated on our drawing form that you had heard about us but had never tried our lingerie or attended a Lacy Lady Lingerie party. I would like to offer you an opportunity to hostess your own party. Being a Lacy Lady Lingerie hostess is exciting and profitable. Most of our hostesses earn enough credits to receive their favorite outfit for free! Is there any reason why you wouldn't want to have a few of your friends over for an evening of fun and entertainment?"

Entrant: "Oh, I don't know. I think we are all getting a little too old for that."

Your response: "You are never too old to enjoy yourself, Mary! Many of my clients are much older than you. When was the last time you had your friends over for an evening that will be this much fun? I bet it has been awhile."

Entrant: "My friends are too stuffy. They would be intimidated by the idea of attending a lingerie party."

Your response: "Why don't we give them the chance to decide for themselves? Let's book a date for your party. Then, you can call your friends and invite them to come. You might find that they've been wishing someone would ask them to a Lacy Lady Lingerie party so they would have an excuse to do something a little daring."

Entrant: "Okay, but I'm not promising anything spectacular."

Your response: "Don't worry. I will provide the spectacular. Anyway, I think I would have fun just showing our line to you. You are a very nice person. Which week is better for you, this week or next?"

PROSPECTIVE CLIENTS ARE EVERYWHERE!

Prospective clients are everywhere! From reading this chapter, you now know that you do not have an excuse for earning one dime less than you want to earn. Although prospecting for clients may be a little frightening in the beginning, once you have practiced for awhile, it will become second nature. Besides, if you never leave your comfort zone, you will never grow. I love meeting new people, and have come to enjoy cold calling for clients. In addition to building my business and confidence, I met one of my best friends and coworkers, Patricia Connor, through cold calling using double business cards. That was ten years ago. I have enjoyed the benefits of knowing Patricia for all of these years because I overcame my shyness of talking to strangers.

CHAPTER SUMMARY

• When you are new to direct sales, the best place to begin your business is with friends, acquaintances, coworkers, and family.

• The best thing to do when someone demonstrates disinterest in your business is to drop the subject, and from that point forward, avoid talking about your business with that particular person.

• When prospecting for clients you must be confident at all times.

• Cold calling using double business cards is an effective way to turn strangers into clients.

• Asking your established clientele for referrals is an efficient way of locating prospective clients.

• On days when you must remain in your home, telephone soliciting may be your only means of making new contacts.

• Distributing free product samples, or catalogs, is a great way to meet prospective clients; however, you must follow up with your prospective clients by phone or in person.

• The biggest advantage of door-to-door soliciting is that you can complete your prospecting call and demonstration in one step.

• Networking is one of the easiest ways to locate clients.

• Product satisfaction surveys are an excellent way to meet prospective clients and can be developed and conducted by anyone.

• Participating in trade fairs is a great way to obtain leads provided you hold a drawing for a prize.

• Prospective clients are everywhere.

DIARY TO SUCCESS

CHAPTER THREE

Sure-Fire Techniques for Booking Demonstrations

You are about to read the most important chapter in this book, and as such, I want you to promise yourself the following:

1) I will not only read this chapter, I will study it until I fully grasp the principles and techniques outlined!

2) Using my own wording, I will record each principle and technique I learn in the "Diary to Success" at the end of this chapter!

3) I will immediately begin practicing the techniques I learn!

4) I will keep this book with me and whenever I falter while booking, over the phone or at a demonstration, I will refer to my diary and this chapter!

I realize that the opening of this chapter is somewhat out of the ordinary. My reason for starting this way is that I wanted to get your attention. An inability to book appointments is the number one frustration I hear expressed from direct sales people. In the previous chapter on prospecting we learned that potential clients are everywhere! What then is the key to getting clients to book?

Becoming a master at setting appointments requires an understanding of why clients book. Clearly, people book with us because they *feel* they will *benefit* from our products or services. Seems simple, doesn't it? Arranging appointments *is* simple; however, somehow as salespeople we manage to make booking one of the more complicated aspects of business. Let's take a look at how we complicate such a straightforward process.

HOW THINGS GET COMPLICATED

The first mistake salespeople make is in assuming their clients are doing them a great favor by agreeing to see them. *What is forgotten is that we are also doing our clients a favor by agreeing to meet with them!*

The second mistake we make is a direct result of our first incorrect assumption. When we assume we are indebted to our clients, *we forget to sell* our time, self, service, and products; instead, we resort to some rather unique booking techniques. Following, we will explore your relationship with your clients and hostesses. In this way you will see who is actually doing what favors for whom. Once we have done this, we will identify ineffective and effective booking attitudes and techniques.

BOOKING...WHO IS DOING FAVORS FOR WHOM?

It is true that when our clients book with us they are giving us their time, and we should always respect our own and others' time! It is also true that when clients buy, we gain profit. Realizing our gains, what do our clients gain when they book with us?

As direct sales people we offer our clients:

1) Superior products. Products marketed directly to the consumer are almost always backed with a company guarantee of total client satisfaction. Your company's guarantee should give you utmost confidence in your product. Whenever you find yourself doubting your product or service, simply ask yourself, "How would it be possible for a company to stay in business, and offer a 100-percent guarantee of total client satisfaction, if its products were not superior?" The truth is that the direct sales company you are with would have been out of business within a number of months after opening its doors if it did not have superior products. So relax, you are marketing a fantastic product!

Adding to your confidence that you are marketing a superior product should be your own, and your ever-growing list of happy clients', satisfaction with your products and service. Never, never let your experience with one or two dissatisfied clients lead to you to doubt your products! The purpose of your company's guarantee is to ensure your clients' satisfaction by exchanging faulty or incorrect products, or when necessary, refunding their purchase price. You will never be able to satisfy everyone's needs, so don't panic when you cannot satisfy some clients. Dwell instead on the incredible number of satisfied clients you have and will have! We will discuss this more when we cover client service as a way to skyrocketing profits.

2) Our time. Our clients invest their time when they book with us and

we invest our time when we travel to see them. By seeing our clients in the comfort of their homes or offices, we save our clients valuable time and money.

3) Competitive prices. When our clients shop with us they buy at competitive prices, while still receiving superior products and services.

4) "Free" expert information. It is quite likely that part of your service includes tips on how your clients can receive maximum use and benefit from your products. You invest your time, energy, and expertise, free of charge! Wow!

So who is the real winner? You, your client, or both of you? I say, in direct marketing, both the business person and the client win, with the scales tipped in favor of the client. So how do we get fooled into believing our clients are doing us a favor when they book, forgetting we are also doing them a great service? We get trapped because we forget how wonderful our products and services are and we forget to *sell* what we offer! I'll get back to this point in a minute. Right now, let's take a look at what we offer our hostesses for inviting their friends to a group demonstration.

FAVORS WE DO FOR OUR HOSTESSES

I deal with what we offer our hostesses separately because I know how easy it is for business people to forget how absolutely wonderful it is to be a hostess.

When our client agrees to hostess a group demonstration:

1) She will receive superior products, superior service, competitive prices, and free expert advice.

2) She will spend an evening with her friends. Keeping in mind how little time people take to pamper themselves, this is a real treat.

3) She will be the center of attention all evening and will be thoroughly spoiled by you, especially after you have started practicing the principles outlined in the chapter on coaching and caring for your hostesses.

4) She will earn the group's esteem for having had the brilliance to introduce them to you and your amazing products, service, competitive prices, and expertise.

5) She will receive a thank you gift from you...everybody loves presents.

6) She will earn products and/or prizes for sales and future bookings obtained by you at her demonstration.

7) Most importantly, she and her guests will have fun!

FAVORS HOSTESSES DO FOR US

Now, you may be saying to yourself, "That all sounds very impressive, Joy, but my hostess still has to clean her house, bake goodies, and invite everyone to attend. I am asking her to do a lot for me and she deserves everything I give her!" You are right. Your hostess is very special and she deserves everything you give her; however, you are very special too! Think for a moment...your hostess's house must be cleaned anyway; she has probably been looking for a reason to get together with her friends, which she never seems to have the time to do; and baking for friends is enjoyable.

I don't mean to make things seem too simple; however, I do want to make the point that our *clients and hostesses win when they book with us!* Balanced on a scale, the list of benefits to us, compared to our clients and hostesses, would look like this.

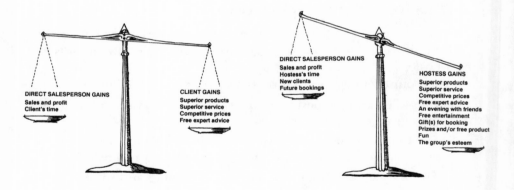

Clearly, when we weigh the benefits of booking, the scales are tipped in favor of our clients and hostesses. Let's take a further look at how we complicate booking.

When we forget how wonderful we, our products, and our services are, we begin to do rather strange things. I remember all too vividly how incredibly creative my first booking techniques were. I remember because, in spite of all of my cautions against doing so, I still see Camelion consultants using the very same creative techniques. Perhaps you are aware of the techniques I am talking about: the coercing technique, the bribing technique, and the begging technique. In case you are unfamiliar with these techniques, I will give you some examples.

INEFFECTIVE BOOKING TECHNIQUES...IS THIS YOU?

The Coercing Technique

"Oh Mary! You are my very best friend. If I can't count on you, who can I count on?"

I used this technique when I was new to direct sales. It actually worked on my mother, sister, and best friend...they love me. Once, and only once, I even applied this technique at a group demonstration. Standing erectly at the head of the dining-room table, I systematically embarrassed myself and each of my hostess's guests as, round robin style, I harassed each woman with, "You want to have a party for me, don't you? No! Well, how about you? You would be a good hostess! No!" Needless to say, I quickly abandoned the coercing technique.

The Bribing Technique

"I really want you to be my hostess. You can win a lot of prizes. I'm offering everyone a 10 percent discount this month. I'll buy all of the refreshments. I'll even help you clean the house!"

Okay, I never used the bribing technique to the extent of the above example. I hate cleaning house and I would probably eat all of the refreshments before I arrived at my hostess's home. I have, however, tried bribing with prizes and discounts. The problem here is that you are bribing your hostess, rather than getting her excited about what you, your products, and services can do for her and her guests! If your hostess does not believe her friends will be excited about attending a demonstration, she will hardly be concerned about discounts and prizes she can win from the sale of products no one is likely to buy. Besides, without being excited about her group showing, how will your hostess get her friends excited about attending...by bribing them too? This type of booking can become very costly, and we are in business to make money, not give it away!

The Begging Technique

"Mary, if you just do me this one little favor, I promise I will pay you back. Honest. Please. I'll never ask you for anything again."

This technique was extremely effective on my mother's best friend. I resorted to it when I realized coercion would not work...she didn't love me like my mother does.

The problem with the begging technique is much the same as the problems with the other techniques we have explored thus far. Our trickery may result in some bookings, but what tools do these techniques give our hostesses for getting their friends to attend? How can your hostess get friends excited about going to her group showing if you haven't managed to get her excited?

THE S.W.I.F.T. PRINCIPLE

Have you ever wondered why we are called "salespeople" as opposed to "beggars," "bribers," or "coercers"? We are referred to as salespeople because we are supposed to sell ourselves, our services, and our products!

Earlier I stated that clients book because they feel they will benefit from our products or services. Hostesses book for the same reason. When a client or hostess feels she wants or needs what you offer—in other words, you have sold her on the benefits and features of your products and services—she will book! The technique of getting your clients and hostesses excited about what you offer is called the S.W.I.F.T. principle.

The secret of the S.W.I.F.T. principle—the "So What's in It For Them" principle—lies in getting your clients and hostesses excited about what they stand to gain by booking with you. Notice that I said *excited!* Excitement sells...so get excited, and you will get your clients and hostesses excited! Forget about what your clients are doing for you, and instead, concentrate on what you can do for them, then tell them!

PERSONALIZING THIS TECHNIQUE
TO YOUR BUSINESS

Now that we have abandoned coercing, bribing, and begging as booking tools, and learned the secret of the S.W.I.F.T. principle, let's turn to the "Diary to Success" at the end of this chapter and list the benefits and features of your business's products and services.

We will make five separate lists entitled as follows: 1) Features of my products, 2) Features of my personal service, 3) My products and services...the combined benefits, 4) Benefits to my hostess of having a group demonstration, and 5) Benefits to the guests who attend the group demonstrations.

Don't skip this exercise—it is vital to your booking success! The purpose of compiling the above lists is to have readily available S.W.I.F.T. reference tables. By referring to your lists, you will constantly be reminded to sell your products, services, time, and self when you are booking.

To aid you in compiling your benefits and features lists, I have provided the following examples of what a Camelion consultant would include.

FEATURES OF MY PRODUCTS

Camelion hosiery:

Is knit in an interlocking stitch and will not run.

Is extremely comfortable.

Allows snags to be easily worked out of the fabric.

Comes in twenty-one, or more, basic and fashion colors.

Is available in many sizes.

Is available in many styles.

Is competitively priced.

Is available in cost-saving value packages.

Is backed by a company guarantee of total client satisfaction!

FEATURES OF MY PERSONAL SERVICE

My clients enjoy:

Caring and individual attention.

Personal service in the comfort of their homes or offices.

Expert advice on caring for hosiery to ensure maximum length of wear.

Advice on using hosiery as an accessory to expand, update, and enhance their wardrobes.

Information on current fashion trends and directions.

On-the-spot delivery.

Follow-up service.

MY PRODUCTS AND SERVICES...
THE COMBINED BENEFITS

Combined, my products and services mean my clients:

Can feel confident in the way they look and never worry about a nasty run spoiling the look of their outfits.

Save money by wearing a superior product that will not run, allows snags to be worked out, and lasts longer than regular hosiery.

Can shop in the comfort of their homes or offices, thereby saving themselves valuable time.

Can take their purchases home immediately.

Will be aware of current fashion trends and directions.

Will know how to expand their wardrobes inexpensively by using hosiery and other accessories.

Can take advantage of my value packages because their purchases are backed by our company guarantee.

BENEFITS TO MY HOSTESS OF HAVING A GROUP DEMONSTRATION

My Camelion hosiery hostesses:

Receive a beautifully wrapped thank-you gift.

Enjoy a fun evening with their friends in the comfort of their own homes.

Are treated to an evening of pampering by me.

Can earn a $50 gift certificate.

Learn the art of using hosiery and other accessories to expand, update, and enhance their wardrobes.

Gain the esteem of the group for having the wisdom to book a fashion accessory class with me.

Gain free personalized advice on accessorizing and updating their wardrobes because I work with three of their outfits during my presentation.

As my clients, have access to a superior product, service, and guarantee!

BENEFITS TO THE GUESTS

The benefits to my hostess's guests of attending one of my group demonstrations are:

They will learn the art of using hosiery and other accessories to expand, update, and enhance their wardrobes.

They will learn about current fashion trends and directions.

They will enjoy a fun, entertaining evening with their hostess.

They will meet new people and make new friends.

They will learn about Camelion's wonderful interlocking stitch hosiery and guarantee.

As my clients, they will have access to a superior product, service, and guarantee.

USING YOUR S.W.I.F.T. REFERENCE TABLES

Your S.W.I.F.T. reference tables serve as constant reminders of everything you offer your clients, hostesses, and hostesses' guests. As such, your tables are invaluable booking tools! You will soon discover that by glancing at your S.W.I.F.T. tables whenever you are booking, you will cease using techniques such as coercing, bribing, and begging, and instead, sell your services and products.

When booking individual appointments, refer to the first three tables you compiled: "Features of my products," "Features of my personal service," and "My products and services...the combined benefits."

Whenever you are booking group demonstrations, refer to all five lists if you are booking with a potential hostess who has never used your products or services. If your potential hostess is familiar with your line, simply remind her that your products are wonderful. Then, using tables four and five, "Benefits to my hostess of having a group demonstration" and "Benefits to the guests," inform your hostess of what is in it for her and her guests.

Remember, when booking with a potential hostess, you must get her excited about being a hostess, as well as tell her why her guests will want to attend. Hostesses only book when they feel their friends will want to purchase your products. The reason for this is that your hostesses feel they are personally responsible for the success or failure of their group showing. If you have ever overheard people talking about a group showing they held or attended, you will have heard evidence of this fact in statements such as: "Oh yes. We had a great time last night. Mary had a clothing party," or "I'm having a lingerie party, and I'd love for you to come." When clients and hostesses are discussing a group showing, the salesperson's name is never mentioned, just the product line being demonstrated and the hostess's name.

SAMPLE BOOKING CONVERSATIONS USING S.W.I.F.T.

Sample #1

Your approach: "Sandy, it's June, your Kitchenware consultant. Are you enjoying the salad crisper you picked out at Connie's party?"

Potential hostess: "I don't use it much. My family won't eat salad."

Your response: "Your family doesn't eat salad. Perhaps they would eat raw vegetables if they were prepared in advance. A client of mine who was faced with the same problem as you started preparing raw vegetables in advance. She always keeps a supply of washed and prepared lettuce, carrots, celery sticks and cherry tomatoes stored in her crisper. She also keeps a jar of homemade salad dressing next to her crisper. Her family now snacks on salad. You might try doing the same thing." (Always show you are concerned about your clients and their purchases.)

Potential hostess: "I could try that."

Your response: "Sandy, I called you for two reasons. I wanted to make certain you were using your crisper, and I also want to make a suggestion. Before I go any further, though, is this a convenient time for you to talk?"

Potential hostess: "I have one or two minutes before the kids get home from school."

Your response: "I will only take a minute. When I met you at Connie's party I thought that I would really enjoy conducting a Kitchenware demonstration for you and a few of your friends. You are such a nice person, and I noticed that throughout the evening everyone kept asking you for your opinion. Everyone likes and admires you!"

Potential hostess: "Thank you for the compliments, but I don't know if I want to be a hostess for you."

Your response: "I don't want you to be a hostess for me, I want you to be a hostess for yourself. Let me tell you some of the benefits my hostesses receive. First of all, you will have an evening of fun and entertainment with your friends. If you are like most women, you do not spend enough time doing the things you really want to do. Secondly, you will receive a booking gift, and when two of your friends book showings of their own and when your total show sales are $200 or more, you will win Kitchenware's gift of the month. This month we are giving away a complete patio serving set worth well over $100 retail."

Potential hostess: "I thought Connie won a set of table lamps."

Your response: "She did. Last month Kitchenware rewarded our hostesses with table lamps. This month we are giving away patio serving sets. Variety is one of the features that keeps our clients coming back, year after year. This brings me to my next point. I am certain most of your friends have not recently had an opportunity to attend a Kitchenware par-ty. Most of them probably are not aware of our new fashionable, clear, stacking canisters. I know you were impressed with our new containers. In fact, I'm sure I remember you saying that you would like a set for yourself."

Potential hostess: "You are right. I did say that."

Your response: "Sandy, is there any reason why you couldn't have a few friends over and hostess a Kitchenware party? I know you will be glad that you did!"

Potential hostess: "I guess not, but it will have to be a Wednesday night when my husband is at bowling."

Note: Whenever you call your clients, it is important that you show you are concerned about them and the products they have purchased from you. Never be afraid that your clients may be dissatisfied; instead, see each encounter with your clients as an opportunity to ensure they are satisfied with their purchases. Remember, your company's guarantee gives you the freedom to make certain your clients are happy. So relax, and make a point of working with your clients until they are 100 percent satisfied.

Sample #2

Your approach: "Susan, it's Vicky calling, your Beautiful You Cosmetics consultant. How are you, and how are you enjoying your new skin care?"

Potential hostess: "I'm terrific and I am using my skin care everyday!"

Your response: "I'm pleased. You will be glad you followed your skin care program when you are a few years older. You have such wonderful skin. Susan, I am calling you for two reasons. One was to ensure you were following the program I prescribed for you; the other is to follow up with the suggestion I made when we did your facial. Before I go any further, though, is this a good time for you to talk?"

Potential hostess: "It's a great time. Go ahead."

Your response: "Susan, do you remember that I told you one of the services I offer is to teach glamor to small groups of women?"

Potential hostess: "Yes, you did mention that."

Your response: "You have a good memory. Susan, I have some time available later this week and I would really like to get together with you and four or five of your friends. I know everyone will enjoy the opportunity to use new colors and learn new makeup techniques. I can hardly wait to tell you the suggestions I have for doing your eye makeup. Of course, for having your beauty class, you will be eligible for hostess discounts and receive a special thank-you gift. The real reward, though, is in the fun of the evening and in your friends' appreciation of you for inviting them to your class. I know you will be a great hostess. Is there any reason why you couldn't hostess a glamor class one day this week?"

Potential hostess: "I couldn't this week. Maybe one day next week."

Your response: "Next week will be great!"

AN IMPORTANT WORD OF CAUTION

Even when we are aware of the ineffectiveness of bribing, coercing, and begging—and the incredible effectiveness of the S.W.I.F.T. principle—it is easy to slip into one of the former three when we feel challenged by our clients. Don't make this mistake!

Should your potential hostess or client ask a question or raise an objection during your booking presentation, answer it completely before going on and without becoming defensive. Objections are questions and should not be mistaken for disinterest. We will cover this point in greater detail toward the end of this chapter.

Now that we have explored booking attitudes that do not work and gained an understanding of the S.W.I.F.T. principle, let's take a look at booking techniques that do work!

The seven booking techniques we will cover next are extremely effective when used correctly and consistently. When learning new techniques, it is not enough simply to read them. Your ability to remember and utilize each will be greatly enhanced when you: 1) read each technique and sample at least three times, 2) write each technique, word for word, in your "Diary to Success," and 3) begin practicing each technique immediately.

Please don't skip this exercise, or any of the exercises in this book. You purchased this book because you want to be the best business person you can be. Do yourself and your business a favor by completing each exercise and adopting the techniques outlined.

BOOKING TECHNIQUE #1
—APPOINTMENT DATES

The purpose of this technique is to secure an appointment date the first time you ask for a booking. A common mistake salespeople make when booking is to ask, "When do you think we could get together?"

This is an open-ended question and leaves your client or hostess the opportunity to say, "I don't know. I will get back to you."

If you do not secure an appointment date the first time that you connect with your client, you cannot be certain the appointment will ever take place. Think too how much time is wasted when you must recontact your client two or three times to secure a date.

The technique for establishing an appointment date simply involves asking your client a series of closed-ended questions until an agreed date is decided upon. Study the following samples.

Sample #1

Once you have established your client's interest in seeing your product, say:

"Which would be better for you, this week or next?"

"Next week. At the beginning of the week or the end of the week?"

"The end of the week. Thursday or Friday?"

"Friday. Morning, afternoon, or early evening?"

"Early evening. Which would be better, five or six o'clock?"

Sample #2

"I have some time toward the end of this week. Which would be better for you, Friday or Saturday?"

"Saturday. During the morning or early afternoon?"

"Early afternoon. Great! One or two o'clock?"

Sample #3

"I will be in your area tomorrow. Which would be better for you, sometime in the morning or early afternoon?"

"The morning would be best. Would nine o'clock or ten o'clock be better?"

Note: In addition to ensuring you establish a time to meet with your clients, the technique for establishing an appointment date allows you to control your time.

You can control your time by giving choices that are best suited to your schedule. If you cannot meet with your client on Tuesday, for example, simply do not give Tuesday as a possible choice. When you ask, "Which time this week would be better for you, the beginning of the week or the end?" and your client responds with, "The beginning of the week," simply make your next choices Monday or Wednesday, never giving Tuesday as a possible choice.

BOOKING TECHNIQUE #2
—REVERSE PSYCHOLOGY

When we were small children, our parents taught us to say no whenever we are approached to buy something. Knowing this, we should not be surprised that our clients sometimes respond negatively before they have even heard what we have to offer. The reverse psychology booking technique involves letting your clients answer with their preprogrammed answer of no, and still obtaining the response you want. Study the following samples.

Sample #1

"Mary, I would really enjoy having a Network Marketing demonstration with you and your friends. Everyone loves our products and we really do save our clients money. Is there any reason why you couldn't invite a few of the couples you know over to your house one evening and hostess a demonstration of our wonderful products? I know you will be glad you did!"

Note: When you preface a question with, "Is there any reason why you couldn't…?" and your client says no, her favorite response, she is really saying yes.

Sample #2

"Ellen, I am looking forward to getting your opinion on our wonderful lingerie line. Is there any reason why we couldn't get together one day this week so you can tell me what you think?"

Note: Again, when your client answers with no, she is really saying yes.

When using the reverse psychology technique it is very important that you do not speak after you have asked a question beginning with, "Is there any reason why you couldn't…?" The general rule is, *speak again, before your client has a chance to answer, and you are begging!* Give your potential client or hostess time to think and you will be surprised how often she will say no, which in this case really means yes.

BOOKING TECHNIQUE #3
—BOOKING GROUP DEMONSTRATIONS
FROM GROUP DEMONSTRATIONS

One of the main differences between an experienced direct sales person and a new consultant is that the former knows the value of booking group demonstrations from group demonstrations. Nothing is more frustrating than running the gamut with booking your friends, relatives, and coworkers, only to find, once through, that you are out of leads and out of business! Of course, you have read the chapter on prospecting and know it is quite possible to build a business through leads from trade fairs, referrals from satisfied clients, etc.; however, these methods require a further time commitment. Why not book future group showings at the close of every group showing you conduct? This way you are making profit while you are booking.

There are three more advantages to booking when you are closing with individuals at group demonstrations. 1) Having just purchased your product or service, your client is excited and more likely to book! 2) When you book with someone who has just attended a group showing, she will begin inviting her guests the next day when she is telling her friends and coworkers about her purchases, thereby bringing higher attendance at her showing. 3) It is easier to book when you are face-to-face with your client than over the phone. In person, you can gauge her reaction to your questions and respond appropriately, bringing a higher success rate!

Following is the technique for booking future group showings from group demonstrations. *Read it, study it, and memorize it!* That is right! You must memorize the following technique until you can recite it without thinking.

Memorize This Technique!

"Lea, at each group demonstration I hold, I always select one or two people that I would most like to have as my future hostesses. Tonight I have chosen you because you are a lot of fun to be with and everyone really likes you. I know you would be an excellent hostess. Is there any reason why you couldn't have a few friends over and hostess an accessory party of your own? I know you will be glad you did!"

There are actually three crucial steps involved in the technique for booking group demonstrations from group demonstrations. Let's break down the above sample into the three steps.

Step #1

"Lea, at each group demonstration I hold, I always select one or two people I would most like to have as my future hostesses."

Step #1 tells your potential hostess she was *selected* as a potential hostess. Everyone likes to be selected or chosen, seeing this as a compliment. Because we are flattered when we are selected, your potential hostess's interest will be piqued and she is more likely to hear and consider your proposal.

Step #2

"Tonight I have chosen you because you are a lot of fun to be with and everyone really likes you. I know you would be an excellent hostess."

In step #2, you tell your potential hostess why you have selected her and that you feel she would be an excellent hostess. Before seriously considering hostessing, your client must feel she will be a great hostess. No one wants to do something they do not feel they will be successful at. Remember, hostesses feel responsible for the success or failure of their group demonstrations!

Step #3

"Is there any reason why you couldn't have a few friends over and hostess an accessory showing of your own? I know you will be glad you did!"

It is imperative that you end your booking request with the reverse psychology booking technique. You want your hostess to think, "Why not hostess a demonstration?" while still feeling comfortable to answer with her preprogrammed "no" response which really means yes.

Do you have to use the exact words in the example? Yes and no! The first thing I would like you to do is memorize the technique for booking group demonstrations from group demonstrations, word-for-word. You should be able to recite this technique almost without thinking. Once you are able to do this, you may feel free to substitute your own words.

The reason I want you to memorize this technique before taking literary license with its content is to ensure that you are comfortable using it and that you do not omit any of the three important steps. Once you are easily able to recite this technique, you will quite naturally be able to substitute your own words and order. Should you try to improvise your own words before you have memorized the technique, you will likely alter the technique to the point of ineffectiveness.

Let's take a look at some possible variations to this technique.

Variation #1

"Julie, I would so love to have you as one of my future hostesses. You are fun to be with and I really enjoyed meeting you this evening." (Here you are complimenting your client and telling her you would like to have her as your hostess.)

"I make a practice of selecting my future hostesses from the people I meet at my group showings. Tonight I selected you because I like you and I know you would be an excellent hostess!" (Here you are telling your client she has been selected and that you believe she would be an excellent hostess.)

"Is there any reason why you couldn't have a few friends over and hostess a group demonstration of your own?" (You must end with the reverse psychology technique.)

Variation #2

"Tom, you can see that everyone wants to know about making wine and beer. Tonight, everyone ordered our Best Brew kit. The guys are happy because they have a new hobby and their wives are happy because they save a little money when entertaining. Well, what I am going to suggest is that you get a group together and host your own demonstration. You would be a great host! You could invite all of the guys from the plant where you work." (Here you are telling your potential host that you would like him to have a group showing and suggesting he invite the fellows from where he works.)

"I'm asking you because you get along with everyone. The group looks up to you. When I select a host, I always look for someone who leads the group, and you do! You would be a great host and you could earn a few extra wine and beer mixes." (Here you have told your host why he was selected and, as added incentive, what is in it for him to get a few friends together.)

"Is there any reason why you couldn't have a few of the guys over and host a showing? I know everyone will be glad you did!" (Always end with the reverse psychology booking technique.)

A final word on varying the technique: You can see from the above variations that the order of the technique for booking group demonstrations from group demonstrations can be altered. What is important when using this technique is that you include the three parts outlined above, always ending with the reverse psychology booking technique.

BOOKING TECHNIQUE #4
—TENTATIVE BOOKING DATES

The tentative booking date technique is an effective format for booking group demonstrations when your potential hostess is unsure of when she can have her showing. Quite often a potential hostess will say,

"Sure. I will have a party, but I don't know when. I'll call you." Remember, you do not have a booking until you have an exact date and time for the showing.

Once you know the correct technique, it is quite easy to obtain a tentative booking date from a hostess. It is important to note that tentative dates, more often than not, hold! To ensure that they hold, it is imperative that you coach these "tentative" hostesses with the same care that you coach hostesses with confirmed dates. For more information on coaching, read the chapter on coaching your hostess.

Simply, the tentative booking date technique involves asking your hostess to choose a date that she feels is a good possibility. The understanding is that should your hostess discover that the date will not work for her, she can change the date. The advantage of this technique is that you have a tentative date which will likely hold, and if it doesn't, you can easily move the showing forward.

Sample #1

In response to your hostess who says, "Sure, I'll have a party for you, but I'll have to check my calendar first":

"Wanda, we can wait until you have a chance to check your calendar if you like; however, I have a suggestion which will help us both. Why don't we pick a tentative date to have your showing? Our understanding will be that should the date we choose not be convenient for you when you check your calendar, we can change the date. In this way, I am certain to have at least a tentative date reserved for you, while still having the flexibility to work around your schedule."

Note: When booking, never be afraid to let on that your schedule is busy. Clients want to deal with successful people and if they think you are always available, they will not be favorably impressed.

Sample #2

In response to the hostess who says, "I'm so busy right now. I'll have to get back to you with a date":

"Sue Anne, I know you are a busy lady. That is why I asked you to hostess a clothing party. Busy people always get the most done, so I know you will be a great hostess. More importantly, busy people are always putting everyone else first, forgetting to take time to pamper themselves. Why don't we do this? Why don't we choose a tentative date about two weeks from tonight? If it turns out your busy schedule won't allow you to take an evening for yourself, we can change the date. The advantages are that you are scheduling some time for yourself and I will have a date reserved especially for you! I am quite busy, too, and I wouldn't want to find I was completely booked when you wanted your class."

Sample #3

In response to your hostess who says, "I'll have a party for you, but I'll call you back sometime later this month. I couldn't possibly have it before next month":

"Next month would be great for me too! I am so busy right now, I find myself booking classes six and seven weeks away. Why don't we do this? Let's select a tentative date next month that we both feel will fit in with our schedules. If it turns out that you cannot hold your class on the day we choose, we can move the date; however, we will have the satisfaction of knowing I have at least one date reserved for you."

Note: It is best to book classes to be held within two weeks. This increases the likelihood they will hold; however, when you become proficient at booking, this may not always be possible. It is not uncommon to find experienced consultants booked three, four, or more weeks ahead. Think of the incredible impression it makes on your hostess when she says, "I'll have to have my class next month," and you respond with, "Next month is good for me too! Actually, I am booked solid this month, so if you did want a class this month, we would have to hope for a cancellation."

BOOKING TECHNIQUE #5 —FRIDAY/SATURDAY

The Friday/Saturday booking technique is used when your hostess responds with, "I would love to have a makeup party, but I'll have to ask the women at work which date is best for them." Remember, you do not have a booking until you have a confirmed or tentative date. Think too how much work your hostess will have to do if first she asks each of her friends which date is best for them, and then must recontact everyone to tell them the date she has chosen. The truth is, when a hostess approaches her friends, she is going to find they all want different dates. In the end, she will be forced to choose her own date. She will have done a lot of extra work for nothing. The Friday/Saturday booking technique is designed to save your hostess a lot of unnecessary work and to ensure that you obtain a tentative date.

Sample

In response to the hostess who says, "I would love to have a party for you, but I'll have to check which date is best for the women at work":

"Lorelei, you can check with the women at work if you like, but I have an idea that will save you a lot of extra work. Why don't we select a tentative date that will work for both of us. Then, if you find that the date is not convenient for your coworkers, we can change the date to one that will work.

"I will tell you why I suggest this. Let's imagine you were having a regular house party and you were trying to decide if you should hold your party on Friday or Saturday. What you would find when you called your friends would be that half would want the party on Friday and the other half would choose Saturday. In the end you would have to choose one or the other and most people would make it on the date you chose! You would have done a lot of extra work for nothing. The same principle applies here. You will never get all of the women at work to agree to one date, and in the end you will have to decide.

"Chances are that the tentative date we select will work for most of the women in your office and we will save you the work of having to recontact everyone two or three times. Don't you agree that this is the best thing to do?"

Note: Citing the example of choosing between Friday and Saturday for holding a house party allows your hostess to identify with what you are saying. Most people have held a house party and are familiar with the impossibility of pleasing everyone. They will also remember that, although they ended up choosing one date over the other, most people were able to make their party.

BOOKING TECHNIQUE #6
—BOOKING GROUP DEMONSTRATIONS
FROM INDIVIDUAL APPOINTMENTS

The *key* to booking group showings from individual appointments is to *sell your service!* Study the following samples to see how to do this.

After you have completed your sales demonstration and taken your client's order, say one of the following.

Sample #1

"Rhonda, another service I offer is to come into your home and conduct a demonstration for you and a small group of your friends. There is so much more I would like to show you about our products. There are numerous ways to utilize the items you are taking today and many other products I would like to show you. I know you can't possibly take everything you want today, and by having a group showing, you will earn many of the products you still need. Is there any reason why you couldn't have a few friends over and hostess a group demonstration? I know you will be glad you did!"

Sample #2

"Julie, I know you are going to love your new makeup and skin care line. Another service I offer is to come into your home, and for a group of four or five women, I will give you a free glamor class. Women love glamor classes, and there is so much I want to teach you. I would love you to be my model during your class. Is there any reason why you couldn't invite a few friends over and have a glamor class? I know you would be a terrific hostess."

Sample #3

"Lannie, another service I offer is to put on a small fashion show for you and a group of your friends. You can be my model. We will experiment with different outfits and ways to accessorize each. We will have a ball! There is no charge for this service. Is there any reason why you couldn't have a group of women over and hostess a fashion show? I know you will be glad you did!"

Sample #4

"Kathy, another service I offer my Kitchenware customers, and their friends, is to demonstrate the numerous ways to utilize our products. There is so much more I can teach you about food storage and space-saving utilization. Of course, you will earn prizes and percentage discounts, but the real fun is in getting together with your friends! We'll even play a few games so everyone has a great time. Is there any reason why you couldn't get a group of ladies together for an entertaining and educational evening? I know you will be a fantastic hostess!"

Notice that each sample begins with, "another service I offer is…," and is then followed with a description of what the service includes. Note too that each sample ends with the reverse psychology booking technique, "is there any reason why…?"

The above points are key factors in successful booking. When you promote your group demonstrations as a *service* you are in effect *selling your service!* Remember, we should always sell our self, service, time, and products.

Ending with the reverse psychology technique allows you to remain confident and professional. Never end a booking technique with something such as, "Do you think you would like to...?" or "Does that sound like something you would like to do?" When booking you must appear confident that, of course, your client will want to have a group demonstration—everyone does! Again, you are selling your service and self.

BOOKING TECHNIQUE #7—TURNING INDIVIDUAL APPOINTMENTS INTO GROUP DEMONSTRATIONS

Quite often consultants find it easy to book individual appointments, but hesitate when it comes to booking group demonstrations. The technique for turning individual appointments into group demonstrations works well for consultants who are inexperienced at booking.

To put this technique into practice, once you have booked an individual appointment, simply suggest your new client have a few friends join her for your demonstration. Then, quickly outline a few benefits to her for doing so. Study the following examples.

Sample #1

"Louise, I am so excited that you decided to have a facial. I know you will love our wonderful skin care and makeup line. You know, should you decide that it would be fun to have a few friends join you, I would be pleased to bring along a couple of extra makeup trays. It's exciting to learn with your friends. Louise, can you think of a few special people you would like to invite to join us?"

Sample #2

"Tom, I will be at your place Thursday night at six o'clock. I know you will really be impressed with our new beer and wine making kits. All of my friends are saving money and having a great time experimenting with different wines and beers. You know, Tom, it would be a great idea for you to invite a couple of the guys to join you...maybe a few fellows from work? You would all have a chance to spend some time together, and I know your friends will be just as curious about our system as you are. Should one or two of them decide to take a kit for themselves, I'll give you a little something. Of course, you'll have the benefit of sampling their home brew too! Won't that be fun? Tom, can you think of a few fellows you'd like to have over?"

Sample #3

"Audrey, I am very excited about showing you this year's Christmas decanters. Sometimes I can't decide which I like more…our perfumes or our perfume bottles. Our festive season glamor products are equally beautiful. Friday morning is our agreed-upon time to meet and I am truly looking forward to seeing you again. Audrey, I would be pleased to bring a few extra booklets and samples with me, should you decide to have a couple of the neighborhood ladies join us for coffee. I don't know about you, but I always find shopping with friends is so much fun. Can you think of a few special friends you would like to have over while I am there?"

Notice how casual is the technique for turning individual appointments into group demonstrations; and yet, your hostess still learns the benefits to her for having a few friends over. Note too, although somewhat different from our traditional reverse psychology technique, the closing statement in each sample is designed to elicit a positive response.

This completes our section on booking techniques that do work. The remainder of this chapter is dedicated to booking excuses most commonly used by hostesses and the answers to them. Remember, before you continue, you should record each of the seven techniques we have covered in your "Diary to Success." Just reading these techniques will not ensure your proper use of them. Writing each technique will help, and your ability to use each effectively will increase in direct proportion to how often you review what you have learned. Be patient! It will take you a while to become completely comfortable with all of the techniques so you can readily decide which one will best fit each booking situation you encounter.

COMMON BOOKING EXCUSES
AND YOUR ANSWERS

Booking is a form of selling. You are selling the benefits of holding a group demonstration. As such, you should not be surprised that you may be met with questions, excuses, or objections to holding a group showing. In the same way that you are prepared for sales objections, you must be prepared with answers to booking objections.

Following are booking excuses most commonly used by hostesses. Study each example until you are completely comfortable with it. Remember, when selling, we must appear confident and natural, so you will want to practice each response until you can use it with ease. To help you become familiar with each response, again, I recommend you record each one in your "Diary to Success."

Sample #1

Response: "I would like to hostess a lingerie party for you, but I don't know when I could."

Answer: "Nanette, I realize you are not certain which date is best for you. I am booking up rather quickly, though, so I do not want to postpone reserving a date for you. Why don't we choose a tentative date that we both think will work with our schedules. In this way, we know I have at least one date reserved for you. If something happens and our original date will not work, we can simply reschedule."

The statement, "I would like to hostess a party, but I don't know when I could," is the most frequent booking response. Considering this, you will want to be prepared with your counter response to this statement. We covered this point earlier when we studied the tentative booking technique; I have also included it here because learning to overcome this objection is vital to your booking success!

Note that the consultant's response acknowledged the fact that Nanette was not certain which date was best for her to hold a group showing. By rephrasing what Nanette said, she was letting her hostess know that she was listening to her. Next, she sold her time and self by stating that she books up quickly. Finally, she suggested a plan of action that took all points into consideration…a tentative date for her demonstration! When answering the statement, "I would like to have a party, but I don't know when I could," all three points mentioned must be addressed: acknowledge that you are listening, state that you book up quickly, and suggest a tentative date. Go back and study this example again, paying special attention to the flow of the conversation.

For those of you who are thinking, "That is all fine, Joy, but now I have a date book that is filled with tentative dates which will likely postpone"…relax! *Once you have agreed on a tentative date, your next step is to coach your new hostess just as you would a hostess with a confirmed date booked.* Provided you coach your new hostess properly, you will find as many tentatively booked dates hold on the day they were originally scheduled as do confirmed dates.

Sample #2

Excuse: "Oh, I couldn't have a class for you. Everyone I know is here today!"

Answer: "You must have had a nice time seeing everyone together. I have a great suggestion. Why don't we ask everyone here today to come to your swimwear gathering. I'm certain the guests today couldn't get everything they wanted, and would love to come. An even better idea would be to ask everyone to bring one or two people they know. In this way we will all get a chance to meet new friends. I'm certain, too, that our hostess has a list of guests who couldn't come tonight. We could ask her to invite them to your demonstration. We will have a ball!"

Again, you begin your response by acknowledging your hostess's dilemma. Next, you offer a series of solutions. Finally, you end on a confident note...being certain not to resort to begging, bribing, or coercing.

Sample #3

Excuse: "I couldn't have a class. I don't know anyone!"

Answer: "Oh, are you new in the neighborhood? I have a fun suggestion. Why don't you invite all of your friends from your old neighborhood? I'm certain they would love a chance to see you and your new home. Crystal showings are also a lovely way to meet your new neighbors. We could hold a joint class with your new and old friends. We'll have a great time!"

Sample #4

Excuse: "I can't have a group showing. My house is too small."

Answer: "Don't worry about the size of your home. Some of my best group demonstrations are with intimate groups of three to six people. We'll have a great time. If you like, we could even set up two or three different get-togethers. I know you will be glad we did!"

Sample #5

Excuse: "I can't have people over. My house isn't nice enough." Or "I couldn't have a showing until the renovations are done on my house."

Answer: "Oh, I wouldn't worry about your house. Everyone will be coming to see you, not your house. Besides, I am certain most of them have already been to your place and had a wonderful time visiting with you. Let's go ahead with your showing. I know we will all have a great time!"

Sample #6

Excuse: "I will have a showing, but not until the kids are back in school."

Answer: "Frances, I know what you are saying. Right now life is hectic and busy. I'll tell you what, though—now is probably the time you and your friends need most to take a break. I have a suggestion. Why don't we hire a baby-sitter to look after the kids? I'll even bring a gift for the sitter. Too often, as women, we continually postpone what we like to do. I think that right now is perfect to take some time to pamper yourself. I know your friends will love the idea."

Sample #7

Excuse: "I will have a showing, but not until after Christmas. People are so busy right now."

Answer: "The fact that this is the holiday season is precisely why I am booking so many classes right now. Everyone loves to get together at this time of the year. Hostessing a showing will give you an opportunity to spend an evening with your friends and do some personal and Christmas shopping at the same time! I'm certain you would appreciate the hostess credits. Just think of how much money you will save when you use your hostess credits to pick up a few of our products for gifts, or to pamper yourself! Now is the best time to hostess a showing."

Sample #8

Excuse: "The people I know don't like to go to parties. I couldn't get anyone to come."

Answer: "I understand what you mean. People don't like to get together for a product demonstration party when they do not perceive a need for the products being shown. I think you will agree with me, though, when I say that everyone should know about our fantastic skin care line. You are taking products home with you tonight because you saw a difference in your skin immediately after your facial. Why don't we do this? When you are inviting your guests, stress that you want them to be aware of our skin care line because you think it is the best. Also emphasize that you would really like to see everyone. Let them know that it isn't important that they buy anything. Be certain to tell them some of the things you have learned tonight and that we will be having a class, not a party. I'm positive you will pique their interest, and will end up having a very successful class!"

Sample #9

Excuse: "I'm too busy right now. Maybe later."

Answer: "The fact that you are a busy person is the reason I asked you to hostess a jewelry demonstration. Busy people always get the most done and have the very best gatherings. I have a suggestion. I am booking up rather quickly and I want to be certain when you do decide to have your showing that I have a date reserved for you. Why don't we pick a tentative date for you to spend an evening relaxing with your friends. I'm certain you deserve the break. If it turns out you are just too busy, we can always change the date to a later time."

Sample #10

Excuse: "Everyone I know is away on vacation."

Answer: "Almost everyone I know is away on vacation too! I love this time of year because people are so relaxed and happy. You know, Susan, many people are already back from their summer vacations, and some poor souls don't even get a summer break. Why don't we do something special for them and go ahead with a booking within the next few weeks? This time of year is perfect for early evening showings outside on the patio."

Sample #11

Excuse: "No thank you. I'm not interested."

Answer: "I'm truly sorry to hear you say that. I would love having you as my hostess. Is there a particular concern I could address for you?"

BE PREPARED

You can see from each of the examples above that there is always an appropriate answer to booking objections. The trick is to be prepared and remain calm, cool, and relaxed with your response. Many people believe their reasons for not booking are legitimate, until you take the time to show them a way around their particular problems.

You would never consider simply dropping the topic if after trying to close a sale, a client asked you for further clarification, or the price of your products. You would answer the questions, even if your client asked two or three different questions, then close again. The same principle applies when you are closing a group or individual booking. Simply answer your potential client's or hostess's questions—or objections— and close again!

Remember, you are not being "pushy" when you make suggestions or overcome objections. You are merely supplying missing information and offering solutions to perceived problems. When you believe you are marketing the best products, and know in your heart that you offer a superior service, you should feel totally comfortable doing your best to ensure that everyone is aware of what you have to offer. Making people aware sometimes requires that you overcome objections and offer suggestions!

CHAPTER SUMMARY

• Clients book with salespeople because they *feel* they will *benefit* from our products or services.

• A common mistake salespeople make is in assuming their clients and hostesses are doing them a favor when they agree to an appointment or group demonstration. The truth is that both the client and salesperson win in direct sales, with the scales tipped in favor of the client!

• The incorrect assumption that our clients and hostesses are doing us a favor by agreeing to an appointment, or to hostess a group showing, often results in salespeople resorting to ineffective booking techniques such as coercing, bribing, and begging.

• The key to successful booking lies in utilizing the S.W.I.F.T principle...the "So What's in It For Them" principle.

• The seven effective techniques for booking individual and group demonstrations are:

1) The technique for establishing an appointment date.

2) The reverse psychology booking technique.

3) The technique for booking group demonstrations from group demonstrations.

4) The tentative booking dates technique.

5) The Friday/Saturday booking technique.

6) The technique for booking group demonstrations from individual appointments.

7) The technique for turning individual appointments into group demonstrations.

• Booking is a form of selling; therefore, salespeople should always be prepared with answers to booking excuses and objections most commonly used by potential hostesses and clients!

DIARY TO SUCCESS

CHAPTER FOUR

Ensuring That Demonstration Dates Hold

One of the most costly and frustrating occurrences for any business-person is to book an appointment only to have it cancel or postpone a few days later. There are definite techniques that will greatly reduce the number of cancellations you endure and will assure you of higher profits. Mastering these techniques is crucial to the success of your business, so make a point of reading this section two or three times. Simply understanding the theories for cementing and confirming appointments is not enough; you must master the art of selling your time and service!

SELLING AND CONTROLLING YOUR TIME

How often have you booked a visit with your doctor or dentist, days or weeks in advance, only to find yourself waiting in the front office for fifteen minutes to an hour past your scheduled appointment? Chances are you are as docile as the other twenty patients kept waiting each day and assume you have no alternative but to endure this incredible waste of your time and energy. Why do you wait without saying a word? You wait because you assume the doctor's time is more important than yours. After all, a doctor is an important person and your health and well-being would suffer without his or her services and knowledge.

You are an important person too, and your time is as valuable as your doctor's. There are two things I have learned while sitting in the medical office. One is that I should always arrive at health care appointments with a good book or paperwork that needs my attention. The second is that if the medical profession can sell its services and time so well that hardly anyone complains about waiting to see a doctor, so can I!

Being able to sell your time starts with your attitude toward yourself and the services, goods, and knowledge you offer. In Chapter 3 you were asked to compile lists of the features of your products and personal service. If you skipped this exercise, go back and complete it now. I cannot stress enough how important it is that you are aware of everything you have to share with your clients. In fact, I suggest you keep your features and services list by the telephone whenever you are booking individual or group appointments. You never know when you might need a confidence booster shot. Remember, you must be totally convinced of your business value before you can be fully effective at selling your time and services.

Direct sales companies market superior products and their independent consultants are professionally trained. As such, there is no need for you to hesitate when booking. As a professional business person you offer your clients quality products and expert knowledge. Study the following example to see how you can effectively sell your products, services, and time when booking.

Part #1—Selling Your Products and Services

Consultant: "Janelle, this is Carole. We met at Tom and Sue's party on the weekend. How are you?"

Potential client: "Hello, Carole. I'm great. How are you?"

Consultant: "I am well, thank you for asking. I am calling you for a reason, but before I begin, do you have a quick minute to talk?"

Potential client: "I only have a minute, but go ahead."

Consultant: "I will only take a minute. Janelle, the reason I am calling is tell you a bit about the Inner Beauty skin care and makeup products I market. Have you ever heard of Inner Beauty?"

Potential client: "No. I haven't."

Consultant: "Very quickly then, our skin care products are ophthalmologist and dermatologist tested. They are fragrance free and are sensitivity and allergy tested. We have three different skin care systems to meet the individual needs of every woman. Our products are water soluble, light, natural looking, easy to apply, and backed by a company guarantee of purity and quality! We also have an extensive variety of base makeup, eye-shadow, and blush shades. And guess what, Janelle…our makeup is color coded to enhance the coloring of the four different seasons or skin tones. Isn't that exciting? Have you ever been color analyzed?"

Potential client: "Yes, I have been color analyzed. I think I am a 'winter.'"

Consultant: "You are a 'winter.' I'm a 'summer.' Janelle, you will absolutely love our 'winter' line of makeup shades. The blues, greys, and pinks are fabulous. Janelle, one of the services I offer is to come into your home and do a complete color, skin care, and makeup analysis for you. My clients love this service because they feel more attractive and confident when they know they are wearing colors and makeup which harmonize with their natural coloring."

Part #2—Controlling and Selling Your Time

Consultant: "Janelle, I am really booked up this week, but I do have a few openings left. Which would you prefer, a day or evening appointment?"

Potential client: "An evening appointment would suit me best. Ted could watch the kids."

Consultant: "Great! I am completely booked tonight and tomorrow, but I have one opening Wednesday at seven. How does that suit your schedule?"

Potential client: "I have my bookkeeping course on Wednesday night."

Consultant: "Okay. Let me think for a minute. I have a six o'clock appointment on Thursday night, but I could meet with you at eight o'clock."

Potential client: "Eight o'clock on Thursday would be great!"

Part #3—Continue Selling Your Time

Consultant: "Now Janelle, I have reserved eight o'clock on Thursday night especially for you! Do you have a calendar handy to make a note of our appointment? I am extremely busy these days and I am not certain I will have time to confirm our appointment."

Potential client: "I will mark it on the calendar I use to keep track of my children's appointments. I look at the calendar every day."

Consultant: "Great! Janelle, as well as being something I enjoy doing, servicing my Inner Beauty clients is a business for me. You can count on me to be there, rain or shine. See you on Thursday at eight!"

Did you notice in the above example that Carole continued selling her time even after Janelle said she was taking a bookkeeping course on Wednesday night? Did you notice, too, that Carole did not specify whether she was booked with business or personal obligations? Instead, she simply said she was booked that night and on Tuesday night. There is no need to tell your clients why you are busy. In fact, the less you say, the more control you have over your personal time and the more likely your clients are to assume that you are booked solid with business appointments. This is exactly what you want them to think because clients like to deal with successful businesspeople.

Note: When establishing an appointment date, never insinuate that you have an entire day or numerous times open. Instead, ask your client which time of the day she would prefer to schedule her appointment. Once she has answered whether she prefers a morning, afternoon, or evening appointment, then offer alternative booking dates that you have open. By doing this, you are selling and controlling your business and personal time.

YOUR DATEBOOK—A TOOL TO SELL YOUR TIME

A datebook filled with appointments is one of the easiest ways to sell your time. Even though you may not be booked solid with business appointments, being booked solid with a combination of personal and business obligations is quite easily accomplished. My datebook is a secretary's nightmare. In my datebook you would find business appointments, personal obligations, medical appointments, recreational activities, birthdays, anniversaries, free time, goals, accomplishments, and my most favorite of all...doodling galore. When people catch a glimpse of my datebook, they always comment on the doodling, and on the fact that my book is filled with obligations. They notice that I am busy, and they assume I am important...like the doctor!

Make a practice of noting all of your personal and business obligations in your datebook. The result will be a well-organized life, as well as increased bookings and profits!

CONFIRMING APPOINTMENTS THE RIGHT WAY!

Successfully confirming appointments to ensure they hold requires skill and timing. We've already explored the value of selling your time when you initially book a presentation, and I stress it again here. If you have not adequately sold the initial booking, your confirming skills will matter little.

The first thing to remember about confirming appointments is that not doing so will result in your valuable time being wasted with "no shows." Before I learned the value and method of effectively confirming appointments, I arrived at many doors to find no one home, or a puzzled husband greeting me with the frustrating news that his wife was away.

Questions such as "I was just calling to see if you remembered our appointment?" or "I was calling to see if we are still on for today?" are weak and invite cancellations. The problem with these types of questions is that they intimate that the salesperson does not respect her own time, thereby giving the potential client a chance to make an excuse to cancel or reschedule. As a rule, questions are poor openings for confirming presentations. When you ask a question, your voice generally rises at the end, implying insecurity. And we all know that clients want to deal with confident, successful salespeople.

Statements of fact that are definite and do not invite a cancellation or postponement are far more effective for ensuring that your appointments hold on the day they are booked. Notice how powerful are the following confirmation statements.

1) "Tom, this is Anne. I am just going out the door, and I will be at your place in about one hour!"

2) "George, this is Bob. As promised I will meet you at the diner at six."

3) "Mary-Beth, this is Ruth. I am so excited about meeting with you and your friends at our group showing tomorrow night."

Sometimes it is necessary to ask questions when you are confirming appointments. Before asking a question, though, always remember to make a power statement first. For instance, if you want to ask your hostess how many guests are coming to her showing, begin with a power statement, then ask your question.

Sample

"Annabelle, this is June. I am really looking forward to conducting your showing tomorrow night. I am all packed up and ready to go, and all I need to know is how many guests will be attending."

When you let your hostess know that you are certain the showing is still scheduled and are even ready twenty-four hours in advance, she will be far less likely to cancel or postpone.

Before I started my Mary Kay Cosmetics business, I was a hostess for one of their consultants whose name was Sandra. I will never forget the night she called to confirm our show. Earlier that month I had postponed our initial booking because I had not invited anyone and had lost my enthusiasm to be a hostess. At that point, Sandra had been careful not to act disappointed and instead, rescheduled our showing for two weeks later. This time, instead of calling in advance, Sandra waited until the last possible minute to confirm our showing. A wise woman, she assumed I would not let her down at the last minute. You can imagine the look on my face when I answered the telephone and heard Sandra say, "I'm on the way out the door, I will be there in forty-five minutes!" Again, I hadn't invited a soul, but I never told Sandra. Instead, I hung up from talking to her and immediately called two friends and a neighbor to rescue me. Thank goodness, they came through and my show was a great success. With only four customers in attendance, Sandra sold over two hundred dollars worth of skin care that night!

Waiting until the last minute to confirm individual appointments can be very effective, and in the above case, Sandra was successful in confirming our group showing forty-five minutes before our scheduled time. However, in general, I prefer to confirm group showings twenty-four to forty-eight hours in advance. The night Sandra confirmed with me she was lucky that I was actually home, because I had honestly forgotten our appointment. The fact that I was single was another point in her favor because I did not have to be concerned about preparing dinner for a family. The circumstances might have been quite different with someone else.

PERSONALLY INVITING THE GUESTS

The practice I have found to be absolutely the most effective and profitable in cementing a booking is to call and invite the guests myself. In fact, when I have employed this technique, I have never, and I mean never, had a group showing postpone or cancel at the last minute! Never is a pretty powerful word, so you know how incredibly potent this practice must be.

Before we cover the do's and don't's of inviting the guests yourself, let's take a look at why hostesses postpone and cancel bookings. The most obvious reason is the same reason why I postponed my first group showing, and that was not being prepared. Hostesses are busy people with numerous responsibilities including: working full-time, caring for their families, participating in hobbies and other scheduled activities, helping at their children's schools, visiting with friends and relatives, and attending church activities. When a hostess forgets about a showing she has scheduled with you, she is not deliberately being inconsiderate;

more likely, she has fallen victim to a heavily taxed personal life.

The second point I would like to make is that when a hostess books with you, she is excited about her showing. By the time of her group showing, though, dozens of other obligations and responsibilities have been shouldered onto her. Therefore, it is not surprising that we sometimes find ourselves somewhere near the bottom of our hostesses' priority lists. Understanding the hectic schedules and numerous obligations our hostesses endure, it only makes sense that we help them prepare for their group showings.

Hostesses cancel and postpone for other reasons too. Double booking is a common mistake and one reason why you should always ask you hostess to mark your showing on her family's or children's calendar. Being requested to work overtime by an employer or one of her children suddenly becoming ill are other reasons. I guarantee, though, that if you ensure that the guests are invited well in advance, your hostess will go ahead with her group showing no matter what circumstances might arise.

THE STEPS INVOLVED IN PERSONALLY INVITING YOUR HOSTESS'S GUESTS

1) Book your group showing and ask your hostess to mark your special day on her family or children's calendar.

2) Coach your hostess as to how she can ensure that she has a successful group showing. (We will cover coaching your hostess in greater detail in the next chapter.)

3) Tell your hostess that you would like to help her prepare for her group showing by personally inviting the guests to attend.

4) Once your hostess has agreed to the idea of you inviting the guests, ask her to compile a list of her guests' names and phone numbers. Ask her to have her list ready within the next forty-eight hours; after all, she will want to make certain her guests are aware of her group showing early enough to reserve the date to attend.

5) Call your hostess at the agreed time and ask for her guests' names and phone numbers.

6) Call your hostess's guests as soon as you receive the list and let them know they are invited to attend your hostess's group showing. Also, inform them as to what your presentation entails and why they should attend. In other words, using the S.W.I.F.T. principle, tell them what's in it for them to attend.

7) Two days before your hostess's show, call all of the guests and confirm their attendance.

8) Call your hostess and inform her as to how many guests are coming and ask if she can think of anyone else she would like to invite.

WHAT IF MY HOSTESS DOESN'T
WANT ME TO INVITE HER GUESTS?

The first question I am always asked when teaching the practice of personally inviting your hostess's guests is, "What if my hostess doesn't want me to call her guests?"

Obviously, if your hostess does not want you to invite her guests, you can't! That is why it is imperative that you employ the S.W.I.F.T principle—the "So What's in It For Them" principle—when you suggest to your hostess that you help her invite her guests. Study the following example.

Sample

Consultant: "Susan, I am thrilled that you are going to be one of my hostesses. There is something I can do to help ensure that you have a tremendous turnout at your showing and that all of the guests have a great time!"

Hostess: "What is that?"

Consultant: "Well, one of the things we must do to make sure everyone can reserve your special day is to invite them well in advance. In fact, we should invite them within the next day or two. Perhaps you could even start inviting them at work tomorrow."

Hostess: "I suppose I could do that."

Consultant: "Great. Susan, I also find that the guests really appreciate it when I call and tell them what will be covered at our showing. As well, I like to ask each guest if she has any particular questions or special requirements she would like me to cover at the showing. [Give an example of the kind of questions previous guests have asked you.] For example, a question I am often asked when I telephone guests is, 'Are your products guaranteed?' Of course, the answer is yes. As you can well imagine, your guests will feel more comfortable knowing the answers to these types of questions in advance. I also find that guests feel quite privileged and special because I have taken the time to call and find out their special needs. Keeping this in mind, Susan, can you think of any reason why I couldn't call you within a couple of days and get your guest list?"

Hostess: "No, I suppose not. Should I invite people too?"

Consultant: "Of course! You can also let them know I will be calling. In this way if I can't reach someone immediately, you will have already invited her. Why don't I make a note in my datebook to call you on Wednesday night to get your guest list?"

Hostess: "I won't be home Wednesday night."

Consultant: "No problem. Why don't I call you Thursday night? We don't want to wait too long or people will start booking other obligations and won't be able to be at your showing."

Hostess: "Okay, I'll give you my guest list on Thursday."

Note: Should you call your hostess for her guest list and discover that she has not prepared it as yet, don't panic...simply tell her you will call her the next day!

CALLING YOUR HOSTESS'S GUESTS

Calling your hostess's guests is simple and easy. To avoid spending too much time calling the guests, schedule your calling time around the dinner hour, when most people are home. If you happen to catch someone preparing or eating dinner, simply ask when would be a better time to call her back. My favorite time for calling guests is in the evening between 5:30 and 6:30.

I generally invest two hours calling the guests for each of my showings. The first hour is dedicated to inviting the guests to attend. Then, two or three days before my hostess's showing I re-call all of the guests to confirm that they will be attending. Because it is difficult to reach everyone on the same night, I often spread both my initial calls and my confirmation calls over two consecutive evenings. The first night that I contact the guests to attend, I work from one end of the list through to the other; the second night I work from the opposite end. I repeat this same procedure when I am re-contacting the guests to confirm their attendance. With a maximum of two hours invested, I generally contact 80 percent of the guests!

Now, if you are thinking to yourself that two hours is a lot of preparation time to invest in one group showing, you are mistaken. Not only do I generally contact 80 percent of the guests, but I usually experience an 80 percent turnout of the guests I do contact. Now, considering that I ask each of my hostesses to invite fifteen to twenty guests, my usual attendance at group showings is between nine and twelve guests. On an average each guest spends $30, resulting in show sales over $270! Yes, an extra two hours invested in telephoning the guests is well worth the effort!

Make a practice of inviting all of your hostesses' guests yourself and I guarantee you will enjoy much higher profits.

P.S. When people do postpone or cancel appointments, don't feel victimized...even doctors and dentists get stood up!

CHAPTER SUMMARY

• There are definite techniques that will greatly alleviate the problem and frustrating experience of postponed appointments and group showings.

• As clients like to deal with successful businesspeople it is imperative that you always sell yourself, services, and time.

• Being able to sell your time starts with your attitude toward yourself and the services, goods, and knowledge you offer.

• Your features and services list is a great tool to aid you in selling your services and time.

• Direct sales companies market superior products and their independent consultants are professionally trained. As such, there is no need for you to feel hesitant when booking.

• A datebook filled with personal and business appointments is one of the easiest ways to sell your time.

• When establishing an appointment date, never insinuate that you have an entire day or numerous times open.

• To avoid wasting your valuable time, always confirm your appointments.

• As a general rule, questions are poor openings for confirming bookings. Statements of fact that are definite and do not invite a cancellation or postponement are far more effective for ensuring that your appointments hold on the day they are booked.

• If you must ask a question when confirming an appointment, preface your question with a power statement.

• Personally inviting your hostesses' guests is the most effective way to ensure that group showings hold on the day they are booked.

DIARY TO SUCCESS

CHAPTER FIVE

Coaching Your Hostess for Higher Profits in Fewer Hours

Hostesses want to succeed! What could possibly be more devastating than having all of your friends over for an in-home group demonstration to discover that none of them wants to buy? Think for a moment. When a woman agrees to be your hostess she is really recommending her friends use the same products as she does. She wants her buddies to have confidence in her judgment! Should her guests fail to purchase the products she is endorsing, your hostess feels rejected just as you do when a client isn't interested in your products or services.

In Chapter 3 we discussed the fact that everyone wins when you conduct a successful group showing. Your clients win because they are purchasing superior products and enjoying professional personalized service. Your hostess wins because she earns valuable incentive gifts and the group's esteem for having had the wisdom to book with you. You win because you gain new clients and profits. Considering that everyone benefits when a hostess succeeds, you have an obligation to do everything possible to make certain every group demonstration you conduct is successful.

Considering the points we have discussed, it should be easy for you to realize that you are helping, not burdening, a hostess when you recommend ways for her to have a successful showing.

COACHING YOUR HOSTESSES TO SUCCEED

Though the keys to having a successful group demonstration may be second nature to you, they will not be as obvious to your hostess. Be certain you take the time to cover all of the following points with each of your hostesses, even if she has held a group showing with you before!

Inviting the Guests

1) Advise your hostess that, due to prior and unexpected last minute obligations, some of her guests will not be able to attend her group showing; therefore, she should invite twice as many guests as she would like to attend.

2) To ensure that she is able to plan her showing properly, recommend that your hostess ask her guests for confirmation that they will be attending. Common courtesy dictates that guests advise their hostess well in advance as to whether they will be attending.

3) Coach your hostess as to what she should say when inviting people to attend her group demonstration. Even though your hostess may have attended a showing with you before, she may not know how to get her guests excited about coming to hers. For instance, a hostess who asks her guests to attend a "makeup party" will not generate the same enthusiasm as a hostess who asks her guests to attend a "skin-care seminar" or a "glamor class."

4) Suggest that to be certain her guests have ample notification to reserve her special date, your hostess start inviting her guests immediately.

Details to Discuss with Your Hostess!

1) Inform your hostess as to how long your presentation will last and determine what time she would like her showing to start.

2) Advise her to keep refreshments simple as her participation in the evening is essential. After all, your hostess should be the star of the show!

3) Advise your hostess that you would like to arrive thirty minutes before her guests so that you can arrange your display and prepare for your demonstration.

4) Ask your hostess to write the date of her showing on her children's or family's calendar. In this way she will be certain not to double book her showing, and her family will be advised of the event.

5) Ask your hostess not to serve alcohol or refreshments until after your presentation. Explain to her that when people are drinking or eating they become distracted, which often leads to a lengthened demonstration. As most of her guests are committed to being home at a certain hour, they will not appreciate being kept too late.

**Ensuring that Your
Hostess's Social Is a Success!**

1) Ask your hostess to give you her guest list in advance so that you can personally call and invite everyone to attend. In this way, you can ask each person what she would like to gain from attending the group showing, as well as tell her what you will be covering. Explain to your hostess that guests are flattered when you personally call to invite them and are far more likely to be excited about attending.

2) Once your hostess has agreed to supply you with her guests' names and phone numbers, determine a date, within the next few days, when you can call her for it.

3) Let your hostess know what she will earn or win for having her group showing and explain that your incentive gifts are your way of thanking her for helping you and her friends.

4) Inform your hostess that she may take outside orders from guests who cannot attend her showing. Arrange to send her product order forms and catalogs in advance.

5) Tell your hostess that you want her and her guests to have a great time and will do everything in your power to make certain her showing is a huge success.

6) Finish by telling your hostess that you are looking forward to conducting her showing and reconfirm when you will call her back for her guest list.

COACHING YOUR HOSTESS IS TIME WELL SPENT!

Properly coaching your hostesses and personally inviting the guests will ensure: group showings hold on the day they are booked, greater attendance at shows, and higher profits! Nothing is more frustrating for direct sales people than shows cancelling or postponing at the last minute. Now think for a moment...how can your hostess postpone her showing when the guests are already invited and everyone is excited about attending? She can't and she won't because she doesn't need to postpone her showing. The main reason hostesses cancel bookings is that they have procrastinated and failed to provide their guests with ample notice to attend. By personally inviting your hostesses' guests you

Time spent coaching your hostess is well invested

will totally eliminate this problem. In fact, you will likely increase the number of showings that do hold by 30 percent or more. A 30 percent increase in shows held equals a 30 percent increase in profit!

Personally inviting your hostesses' guests will increase attendance at your group showings because you will get everyone excited about your products and presentation. You will also begin to establish a bond of trust with each guest and as a result, all of them will likely purchase products.

Study the following sample conversation for coaching your hostess once you have established a date and time for her showing.

SAMPLE HOSTESS-COACHING CONVERSATION

Consultant: "Betty, I am really looking forward to doing your show next Thursday. I would like you to do a small favor for me. Would you please be sure that you have marked our special date on your family's calendar? I would feel awful if you double booked us by mistake and your family will appreciate knowing which night you are having guests."

Hostess: "I will do that as soon as I hang up from talking with you!"

Consultant: "Great. Betty, there are a few other points I would like to go over with you. I want to make certain you have the showing of the century and that everyone has a great time. Do you have a few more minutes to talk with me?"

Hostess: "Yes, go ahead."

Consultant: "Before I begin, Betty, do you have a pen and paper handy? I think it will help if you take notes."

Hostess: "I have a pen and paper right here."

Consultant: "Good. Now, we've agreed to start at 7:00. My presentation will take about one hour and fifteen minutes. If it is all right with you, I would like to come about a half-hour early so that I can set up my display before everyone else arrives."

Hostess: "Sure. You will get here about 6:30 then?"

Consultant: "Yes, I will be there about 6:30. Betty, a couple of points about inviting your guests. I recommend you invite twice as many people as you would like to have attend. The reason for this is that some of your guests will not be able to come because of prior commitments. As well, some people will probably have to cancel at the last minute. You know how life can be if you are asked to work overtime or one of your kids gets sick."

Hostess: "I understand."

Consultant: "In fairness to you, I also suggest that you ask people for confirmation that they will be attending. Betty, the next thing I want to go over with you is what to tell your guests when you are inviting them to come. No one will be excited if you simply tell them we are having a makeup party. Instead, tell them a little about our wonderful products. Let them know you are using our skin care and have already noticed a difference in your complexion. Tell them that the reason our line is unique is that all of our products contain mink oil, which very closely resembles the natural oils in our own skin. Let your friends know, too, that my presentation is short, sweet, and informative. Not only will they have fun, but they will learn more about how to care for their skin so they can look younger for years to come. If you like, you can also explain that our company specializes in skin care, not glamor, and that we believe that healthy-looking skin provides the canvas on which to paint a beautiful face. I remember you said that the reason you liked our skin care was that it is simple and easy to follow. You also said that you could see results right away. Tell your friends why you like our products. Of course, you should mention that all of our products are backed by a guarantee of satisfaction!"

Hostess: "So basically, you want me to tell my friends why I am using your skin care line, what you will be teaching at the show, and that your products are guaranteed."

Consultant: "Exactly! Betty, if you are planning to serve refreshments, keep things simple. Your guests will want to visit with you and I want you to be the center of my presentation. After all, it is your night! If you are in the kitchen all evening, you will miss all of the fun. And, one other point about refreshments, Betty. It is a good idea to wait until after the presentation to serve alcohol or food. I find that the presentation just takes too long when people start feeling festive. As most of your guests will have to leave at a set time, we should make a point of finishing on schedule."

Hostess: "Can I serve tea or coffee earlier?"

Consultant: "Of course you can! Betty, there is something I can do to ensure your showing is a great success. I would like to phone each of your guests and personally invite them to attend your showing. You can start inviting them, too; however, I find that people are pleased when I call them in advance to see if there is anything in particular that they would like to learn."

Hostess: "I am not certain if my friends will appreciate you calling them."

Consultant: "Don't worry, Betty. I will simply call, identify myself as the person who will be doing your skin care seminar, and ask them if they have heard of our products. I will also ask if they have any particular questions or problems they would like me to address. They will be pleased, I promise! Just think for a moment. Some of your friends may feel shy about discussing their skin care worries in a group. When I call them ahead of the show, they can share their concerns with me and I can discreetly answer their questions on the phone or during my presentation."

Hostess: "Okay."

Consultant: "Good. Betty, we want to make certain everyone has enough time to reserve our date, so I would like to start calling them right away. Is there any reason why I couldn't call you tomorrow night for your guests' phone numbers and addresses?"

Hostess: "I am going to be out tomorrow night."

Consultant: "Okay, how about the next night?"

Hostess: "Fine."

Consultant: "Betty, you realize that you are going to receive 10 percent of the show sales as my thank-you gift to you for introducing me to your friends. I want you to know, too, that you can take outside orders from anyone who cannot attend your show. In fact, I will send you a few catalogs and order forms today."

Hostess: "That's a good idea."

Consultant: "Well, Betty, that is all that I can think to tell you right now. Do you have any questions?"

Hostess: "No, I don't think so. I will call you if I do."

Consultant: "Great. I will call you the night after next. I am really looking forward to doing your class on Thursday night and meeting your friends. You take care of yourself and I will talk to you soon."

CALLING THE GUESTS

Once you have your hostess's guest list, start calling everyone right away. One of the reasons hostesses postpone is that they procrastinate and don't get everyone invited in time. Don't be guilty of the same error!

Calling the guests is simply a matter of: identifying yourself, stating why you are calling, asking them if this is a convenient time to talk, briefly outlining your presentation, and asking if they have any questions or problems they would like you to cover during your presentation. Sound simple? It is! Study the following sample conversation with a hostess's guest.

Sample Conversation with a Hostess's Guest

Consultant: "Hello, is May there please?"

Guest: "This is May speaking."

Consultant: "May, my name is Joan. I am a representative with The Colors of You. Diane Taylor is having a color-analyzing and accessorizing seminar next Thursday and has included you on her guest list. Has Diane called to invite you yet?"

Guest: "I don't know. I was away all weekend. She probably tried."

Consultant: "I'm sure she did. May, I am calling to tell you about some of the things I will be covering at our seminar on Thursday, but before I begin, do you have a quick minute to talk?"

Guest: "Yes, but just a quick minute."

Consultant: "Great. May, the first thing I would like to ask you is whether you have been color analyzed before?"

Guest: "Yes. I was color analyzed about two years ago. I'm a 'winter.'"

Consultant: "I'm a 'winter,' too. May, I would still like to analyze you again if you don't mind. I find that some of my clients have been categorized in the wrong color. As I have had over forty hours of color analyzing training, I would feel more comfortable having personally analyzed you."

Guest: "You can if you like, but I don't know if I will bother coming. I am sure that I am a 'winter.'"

Consultant: "May, I hope that you do come. As well as color analyzing everyone in the group, I will be demonstrating my line of The Colors of You designer fashion accessories. You will absolutely love our selection. We have silk scarves, belts, hosiery, necklaces, earrings, bracelets, brooches, and anklets that have been especially designed for each of the four color groups. Our accessory line is updated each season, so you are sure to be in fashion. Also, because our accessories are color coded to match your skin coloring, every piece you take home with you will coordinate perfectly with your clothing wardrobe. Shopping with The Colors of You takes the guesswork out of accessorizing. Of course, our accessories are backed by a company guarantee of satisfaction, even if worn!"

Guest: "Are your accessories expensive?"

Consultant: "Not at all. In fact, shopping with us will save you money. All of our accessories will update your current clothing wardrobe, which will alleviate the need for you to buy a lot of new clothes this season. By adding just a few jewelry pieces, you will step right into this year's fashion look. May, you really should join us on Thursday night. I know that Diane is looking forward to seeing you and you will have a great time."

Guest: "What time are you starting?"

Consultant: "We are starting at 7:30. Diane is asking everyone to come a little early so that we will be able to begin on time. My presentation will take about an hour and then Diane is serving refreshments. May, I would like to tell our hostess that you will be there."

Guest: "I'll check with my husband and make certain he can sit with the kids."

Consultant: "Great. Remember to reserve Thursday on your calendar for Diane's seminar. May, I have really enjoyed talking with you and I am looking forward to meeting you in person."

The Best Time to Call

Time spent phoning can be greatly reduced by timing your calls to coincide with when people are most likely to be home. My favorite time to call is early evening during the week. Remember, if you catch someone preparing or eating dinner, simply ask her for a more convenient time to call again.

Another important thing to remember is that should someone other than the person you are trying to reach answer your call, ask him for the best time to call the person you are trying to contact. In this way, you will not waste valuable energy trying to call again at a time when the person you want to speak with is not home.

When calling your hostess's guests, start at the beginning of the list the first night you call, then the next evening begin your list at the opposite end. Altering the time of day which you call can help you catch the last few people on your list at home. Don't despair if you cannot reach everyone on the list—your hostess is contacting people too!

Confirming Your Hostess's Guests

Even though you have already called everyone and invited them to your hostess's showing, it is wise to recontact the guests a few days before the actual event. Once you have contacted at least 60 percent of the guests, call your hostess and let her know who has confirmed. Even if your hostess has completely forgotten about her showing, everyone is invited and the show must go on!

COACHING YOUR HOSTESS
WHEN YOU ARRIVE AT HER HOME

Coaching your hostess in her home just prior to the demonstration is crucial to the success of her showing. Remember, even if your hostess has held group demonstrations before, she will probably be nervous and will appreciate your reassurance that the evening will be successful. Study the following guidelines for coaching your hostess in her home when you arrive a half-hour before the guests.

1) When she answers the door, greet your hostess with a huge smile and warm handshake. If she has been working all day long, or has just finished clearing the table from the family meal, your friendly greeting will be greatly appreciated.

2) Once inside, ask your hostess where she is planning on seating the guests and where you can arrange your display. Make certain you are positioned where you can easily see and converse with all of the guests.

3) Ask your hostess where you can meet with each guest individually after your presentation. Explain to her that some of her guests will have questions that they will not feel comfortable asking in front of everyone else.

Note: Meeting with each guest individually will help you and your clients feel more comfortable when you are closing and booking future showings. For instance, someone may want to postdate a check, or buy something that she cannot immediately afford; however, she will not likely tell you so in front of the entire group. Privately you can make arrangements that meet her needs...maybe even book a group demonstration so she can earn the products she wants. Remember too that you do not need Doubting Dorothys around when you are closing a sale. This potential problem is eliminated when you are away from the group.

4) Ask your hostess if there are any last minute guests or cancellations.

5) Ask your hostess if she has any outside orders from friends who were unable to attend her showing.

6) Ask your hostess who is coming tonight who might enjoy hostessing a group demonstration of their own. It never hurts to know who

are the most likely booking prospects!

7) Ask your hostess who is coming tonight who might appreciate knowing about your company's business opportunity. After all, your hostess is generally familiar with the dreams, problems, and wishes of her closer friends.

8) Ask your hostess if she has ever considered a full-time or part-time business of her own. She will most likely answer, "No!" Regardless of her answer, suggest that she watch you for the evening and see if she thinks she could do what you do. Remember, when you share your business opportunity with others you are not only helping yourself financially, you are helping someone else financially!

Sample Conversation for Coaching
Your Hostess in Her Home

Consultant: "Elizabeth, it really is great to see you. I hope you had a good day."

Hostess: "Actually, today was crazy. I had to work an extra hour and when I got home I discovered that my youngest boy has a chest cold. His father is just putting him to bed now."

Consultant: "That's too bad. I hope he's okay. How old is he?"

Hostess: "He's three. I'm sure he will be fine. You mentioned on the phone that you needed a place to arrange a display. I'm going to be using the dining-room table for refreshments, but I thought you could use the coffee table. If you like, I also have a card table."

Consultant: "The coffee table will be fine. Elizabeth, is there some-where that I could meet with each guest individually after my presentation? I find that some guests feel more comfortable asking me questions in private."

Hostess: "My husband will be in the study. Would the kitchen be okay?"

Consultant: "The kitchen will be great. Elizabeth, are there any last minute guests coming?"

Hostess: "Yes, Susan Drayton is bringing her sister. Mary Larsen called and she can't come. Her daughter has the flu."

Consultant: "I'm sorry to hear that Mary's little girl is sick. Did Mary or anyone else give you any orders that you would like me to take?"

Hostess: "Yes, one of the women from where I work wants me to order a gelatin mold for her."

Consultant: "Great. Elizabeth, as you know, you will earn a complete patio serving set when your show sales are over $200 and two of your guests book showings of their own. Who is coming tonight that you feel might like to hostess a showing of their own?"

Hostess: "Actually Mary said she would like to have a show. She was sorry she couldn't come. Susan Thompson would be another good prospect."

Consultant: "I will call Mary tomorrow. Elizabeth, is there anyone coming who you feel would be good doing what I do?"

Hostess: "Are you asking if I know anyone who would want to sell Kitchenware products? I don't know. Maybe Hazel. She's looking for a job."

Consultant: "Hazel sounded very nice on the phone. She would be good. What about you? Have you ever considered a full- or part-time business of your own?"

Hostess: "Me? No way. I've got my hands full with the kids. Maybe after my youngest starts school."

Consultant: "Elizabeth, most of the women who market Kitchenware have children. One of the bonuses of being in business for yourself is that you can schedule your work around your children. I book all of my classes in the evening when my husband is home to look after the kids. Why don't you just consider the possibility? Watch me tonight and ask yourself if you couldn't do what I do. I am certain you could use the extra money with Christmas only three months away."

Hostess: "Okay, but I'm not promising anything."

Consultant: "You don't have to promise anything. I'll be satisfied if you just consider my proposition. I think you would be a great consultant."

Note: Most direct sales companies offer generous incentives and commissions to consultants who actively team-build. At every group showing you conduct, make a practice of asking your hostess and at least one guest if they would be interested in hearing about your company's business opportunity. I am certain you would appreciate the extra income a senior or management position would generate.

HIGHER EARNINGS FOR
FEWER HOURS WORKED

Coaching your hostess takes time and planning on your part. The question becomes, "What would you rather do—hold one class per week with fifteen guests in attendance, or three classes per week with five guests attending?" Obviously, properly coached hostesses result in higher earnings for fewer hours worked!

CHAPTER SUMMARY

• Hostesses want to succeed!

• Though the keys to having a successful group demonstration may be second nature to you, they will not be as obvious to your hostess. It is up to you to ensure that your hostess knows how to have a great showing.

• Properly coaching your hostesses and personally inviting the guests will ensure: that your showings will hold on the day they are booked, greater attendance at shows, and higher profits.

• Once you have your hostess's guest list, you should start calling everyone immediately.

• Even though you have already called everyone and invited them to your hostess's showing, it is wise to recontact the guests a few days before the actual event.

• Coaching your hostess when you arrive at her home is crucial to the success of her showing. When your hostess answers the door greet her with a smile. Once inside, ask her where you can arrange your display and where you can meet with each guest individually. Also, establish whether there are any last minute guests, cancellations, or outside orders. Ask your hostess who she thinks might be interested in hosting a showing of their own or in your company's business opportunity. Ask your hostess if she has ever considered a full-time or part-time business of her own.

DIARY TO SUCCESS

CHAPTER SIX

The Basics of a Successful Sales Presentation

Today, consumers are educated and value conscious. With an ever-increasing choice of products and ways to shop, long gone are "Dollar Sign Dan's" days of smooth orating and exaggerated product claims. Now, a successful salesperson is her clients' teacher and friend. Through probing and active listening, the role of the salesperson is to determine her clients' needs and wants, and then to educate her clients as to how the benefits and features of her products and/or services can satisfy them.

BE TRUE TO THY CLIENTS...KNOW THY PRODUCTS

In any new business there are numerous things to learn and accomplish. Understandably, many beginning direct sales people feel overwhelmed and a little confused. Gradually though, the basics of business become second nature; the excitement subsides somewhat, and one settles into a routine of booking appointments and closing sales. At this point, it is imperative for a consultant to learn more about the products and services she markets.

Almost every direct sales company provides manuals on sales presentation and product knowledge. What I have noticed over the years is that only new consultants refer to their manuals. As noted above, new consultants are overwhelmed and chances are that they retain very little of what they read and studied early in their careers. In the beginning, this has little impact on a new consultant's career because her sheer enthusiasm closes most sales. Later, when the excitement is gone and a consultant moves away from her warm market of friends and relatives, a professional, honest, informative, and interesting presentation becomes crucial. Product knowledge and the answers to questions most commonly asked—objections—become equally vital.

Direct sales is the marketing method of today. Consumers want educated, honest, friendly businesspeople to market products they need and want directly to them in the comfort of their homes and offices. It might as well be you who reaps the benefits of being on the delivery end of fulfilling consumer needs. However, to be effective and successful you will have to be the best in your field. It is that simple. The information you need is at your fingertips in the form of company manuals, experienced managers, and weekly success meetings. All you have to do is make the effort and take the time to learn. In fact, you should be polishing your sales presentation and product knowledge weekly, even daily.

TEN STEPS FOR AN EFFECTIVE SALES PRESENTATION

Like a good book, an effective sales presentation has an opening, a plot, a series of climaxes, and a close. As well, it totally involves the client, captivating her entire attention and interest.

Step #1—Set the Tone

As a professional, you are responsible for setting the tone when you meet with a client. You can create a mood of caution and tension by appearing hurried and anxious, or an ambience of trust and concern by showing a genuine interest in your client's welfare and needs. It is up to you to establish the way in which you and your client will conduct business. Whether your client will leave feeling as though she has just visited the dentist, or a friend, will largely be determined by how she feels about you and how she perceives you feel about her.

Whenever I think of how a salesperson makes me feel, my thoughts immediately turn to our company life insurance salesman, Jim Mee. Jim has taken care of Camelion's life and health care policies since we started. I wouldn't even dream of changing my loyalties to Jim. Why? Because he is always concerned, always available, and always a friend. For years, Jim has been dropping by for coffee. He is sensitive to the needs of running an office and will "duck out" as quickly as he "ducked in" when we are busy. He never imposes, yet makes himself available. When he senses one of us needs to talk, he listens. In short, Jim gives himself to his clients. In exchange his clients recommend him to friends and increase their own business with him. Jim can be trusted to answer questions accurately and to take care of his clients.

The kind of relationship you will have with each of your clients will be determined by your first meeting. Whether or not you make an immediate sale isn't as important as is the long-term relationship which you are beginning to build. In fact, building a business means building a mutually beneficial relationship with each of your clients.

Set a positive, lasting tone and first impression with your clients by creating a mood of professionalism and caring. Take the time to ask about them. What do they do for a living? Are they married? Do they have children? What is new and exciting in their life since you last met? How was their vacation? Did they buy that new car they were talking about, or get the promotion they were trying for at work? Let your clients know you are listening by commenting on what they are saying. You will do damage by pretending to listen while being preoccupied with other concerns. When you meet with a client, put the world on hold, forget about your fears and making the sale, and spend a couple of quality minutes just talking.

Step #2—Your Opening Remarks

Obviously, you cannot continue conversing with a client all day and must turn the topic to business. The transition from asking about your client to your presentation must be subtle and preserve the tone you have already established. Continually, I mention the S.W.I.F.T. principle, and again it applies here. Changing the topic while maintaining the conversational tone requires keeping your clients' needs and wants foremost in everything you say and do. Study the following samples to see how easily this can be accomplished.

"Samantha, I know your time is valuable, so let me share the highlights of my services with you."

"Before we get started let me give you my business card. I want to make certain you know how to reach me when you need my services."

"I promised you a demonstration, so let me show you our product line."

"Rayna, I could talk with you all day, but I know you really wanted a chance to look at our newest items."

Step #3—Probing

Once you have opened, and before you begin your presentation, it is imperative that you establish your client's need for your products and/

or services. Remember, your client's needs must always be foremost in your mind.

Note: The added bonus of probing to discover your client's needs is that your products' ability to meet the very needs you uncover can be referred to in your closing remarks to cement the sale.

Simply stated, probing for information involves asking a series of open-ended questions. Open-ended questions elicit a full answer and cannot easily be answered with yes or no. Examine the following probing conversation sample.

Distributor: "Katrina, when I first told you about our bottled water kit you said that you drink water straight from the tap. What can you recall hearing lately about our local water in the news media?"

Client: "That our water is safe because they put chlorine in it, and that you should run your taps for thirty seconds before drinking or cooking with water."

Distributor: "That's right. Our drinking water does meet health standards. Why then do you imagine our home bottled water kits have become so incredibly popular?"

Client: "I imagine it is because people are afraid of chlorine. I don't know."

Distributor: "I think that people know that it is imperative that we treat our local water. In fact, the government makes our water safe and our bottled water kit makes it smell and taste great. Tell me, what can you see as the advantages for you and your family to have fresh, great tasting water at your fingertips?"

Client: "I suppose we might drink more water."

Distributor: "Right, and health professionals recommend that we drink a minimum of eight glasses of water per day. Even your kids will turn to the tap instead of soda pop. I can remember when I was a kid we would play outside until we nearly dropped. Then, panting, we would run to the house for water. In those days water tasted so good. It wasn't until I installed my own bottled water kit that I realized how much I missed the taste of cold, clear, odorless, and delicious water. Your kids will love drinking water that has been filtered and so will you!"

Step #4—Your Presentation

You can see from the above sample that your presentation will begin while you are probing.Each time your client gives you an answer, you are pre-sented with an opportunity to inform her as to how your products can fulfill the needs she has identified. An added benefit of this procedure is that your client will know that you are listening. The remainder of your presentation should also involve your client as much as possible. Study the following presentation.

Distributor: "Let's have some fun and find out for ourselves how much chlorine is in the water you and your family are drinking. Why don't we go into the kitchen and attach our counter model to your tap? Then, we can test your drinking water for chlorine content as it is, and after it is filtered."

Client: "How are you going to test it?"

Distributor: "The test is simple. We take a sample of the tap water before it is filtered and a sample after it is filtered. Then we add a few drops of the substance in this little bottle to both. If there is chlorine in either sample, the water will turn yellow. The darker yellow we obtain, the more chlorine there is in the water."

Note: Your presentation can continue as you move to the next room and while you are preparing your demonstration.

Distributor: "Katrina, you will be happy to know that in addition to our counter-top model, we also have an under-the-counter unit which automatically filters your water when you turn on the cold water tap. We also have a model which will filter the water in your entire house.

"With our counter-top model, you simply pull this little shut-off valve when you desire filtered water. Now that I have your counter-top model attached, why don't you try turning the cold water tap on and opening and closing the valve for yourself?"

Client: "That's easy to do. The valve automatically closes when I shut off the tap?"

Distributor: "Yes, it does. Now, remember, you do not want to run hot water through your bottled water kit. And of course, you will want to use filtered water for cooking. Why cook with chlorine? After we have completed this test, why don't we make a pot of coffee with freshly filtered water? You will be amazed at how much richer coffee made with filtered water tastes.

"I've poured water from the tap into the first glass and filtered water into the second. Before I add the solution to each glass, I want you to do another experiment with me. Take the first glass with the direct tap water, close your eyes, and smell the water. Can you smell the chlorine?"

Client: "Yes, I can."

Distributor: "Now take a drink and see if you can taste the chlorine."

Client: "I can taste the chlorine just a little."

Distributor: "Now, repeat the same procedure using the filtered water in the next glass. Notice how refreshing it tastes and smells. Which water do you think you and your family would prefer to drink?"

Client: "The filtered water, of course."

Distributor: "Now watch what happens when I add the solution. See, the filtered water doesn't even have a trace of yellow and the direct tap water is quite yellow! Isn't that remarkable?"

Client: "That is amazing."

Distributor: "Would you mind if I took a look under your sink?"

Client: "Go right ahead."

Distributor: "Thank you. Our under-the-counter unit would attach right there. Can you see where I am talking about?"

Client: "Yes, I can. I guess it would be easier to have the unit out of sight."

Distributor: "It would leave you with more counter space. Katrina, why don't we have that cup of coffee we talked about? When you pre-pare it, you will only need to use about two-thirds of the coffee you would normally use."

Step #5—Your Trial Close

Once you have answered most of your client's questions, and she starts nodding her head in agreement with your answers, it is time to do your first trial close. Your trial close should very subtly ask for the sale. Do not worry if your client continues asking questions, or gives you an objection. Every good businessperson welcomes questions and objec-tions, viewing them as stepping-stones to a successful close, not road-blocks to a sale.

Distributor: "While the coffee is brewing, Katrina, why don't you tell me whether you feel your family would get the most use from our counter-top or under-the-counter model?"

Step #6—Answer Questions Professionally

Client: "How much does each of the units cost?"

Distributor: "Pennies per glass. Before I go into that, though, answer another question for me. Have you ever purchased bottled water from the store?"

Client: "I usually don't think of buying bottled water. But I did buy some once."

Distributor: "Why did you purchase bottled water?"

Client: "It was summer and I was on a diet. I wanted something to drink that was calorie free, tasted good, and was cold."

Distributor: "Do you remember how much you paid for the bottled water?"

Client: "Not really—a dollar or two, I guess."

Distributor: "Imagine if you did remember to purchase bottled water every time you went grocery shopping. Over a period of one year you would end up spending well over one or two hundred dollars. If your family started drinking bottled water, the cost would double. Do you agree?"

Client: "Oh yes, of course."

Distributor: "If you started cooking with bottled water from the store and using it to make coffee, the cost would double again. Before you knew it, you would be lugging jug after jug home from the store and spending three, four, five hundred dollars a year on bottled water. Our counter-top home bottled water kit is just a little over two hundred dollars and has a three-year warranty. Our under-the-counter model is just slightly more!

"Katrina, which would you rather do…spend more than is necessary hauling water from the supermarket every shopping trip, or for pennies a glass, have bottled water at your fingertips?"

Client: "I'd rather have the home bottled water, but I don't know if I can afford it right now."

Distributor: "Let's have that cup of coffee now."

Step #7—Your Second Close

Distributor: "Isn't that the best cup of coffee you have had in years?"

Client: "It is good."

Distributor: "Katrina, would you want a home bottled water kit if I could show you that you can afford to own one?"

Client: "What do you mean?"

Distributor: "Our company has a convenience plan that will allow you to enjoy bottled water today while making minimal monthly installments."

Client: "How much would my monthly payments be?"

Distributor: "What could you afford?"

Client: "I don't know. About thirty dollars per month I guess."

Distributor: "Then that is what your monthly installments will be. Let's fill out the forms."

Step #8—Write Up the Order

Distributor: "Katrina, would you please fill out the top portion of this warranty form?"

Step #9—Ask for Referrals

Prospecting for clients is an integral part of business. After you have written up your client's order, it is quite natural to ask for the names and phone numbers of friends your client feels would appreciate knowing about your products or services. Don't worry if some clients will not give you referrals, as many will.

Note: When asking for referrals, never ask for the names of people who would be interested in "purchasing" your products. Words such as "purchasing" and "buying" are very intimidating. Instead, ask for the names of people your client feels would "appreciate knowing about your service" or "like an opportunity to see your products."

Distributor: "Katrina, I am going to ask you to do me and a few of your friends a great service. Who do you know that you feel would appreciate knowing about our home bottled water kits?"

Client: "I don't like to give out the names of my friends."

Distributor: "I don't either, unless I genuinely feel the people whose names I am giving will benefit as a result. I think you will agree with me that everyone would be more than happy to sample our home bottled water. Don't worry. All I will do when I call is tell them who I am, that you thought they might be interested in trying our filtered water, and ask them if I can stop by. If they are not interested, I will simply thank them for their time and hang up."

Client: "I guess that would be okay. I will give you my sister's phone number and the lady's next door."

Step #10—Thank Your Client and Reinforce Her Purchase

Distributor: "I can't believe where the time goes. I will leave you to get back to your family. Thank you for taking the time to see me tonight and thank you for that great cup of coffee. I know you and your family are going to be very pleased with your new bottled water kit. I bet you will find that everyone in your family starts drinking eight healthy, tasty glasses of water per day."

UNDERSTANDING THE GROUP DEMONSTRATION

Although somewhat less personal, your group demonstration should incorporate the same principles outlined above. Your professional group showing should include: a thank-you to your hostess and a warm welcome to guests; prizes the hostess can earn; an outline of the presentation to come; a brief company history; a top-notch team-building talk; a demonstration of the benefits and features of your products and services—flavored, of course, with how they can meet the assumed and determined needs of the group; a question and answer period; a group close; and an individual close with each guest.

Memorize Your Clients' Names

Welcoming the guests to your hostess's group showing begins when each guest arrives. You should make a practice of greeting each guest with the hostess. Make a point of shaking everyone's hands and memorizing their first names. If you are uncertain whether you heard someone's name correctly, ask for clarification. For instance, if you are not sure if someone was introduced as Marian or Mary Ann, ask her to repeat her name.

For those of you who panic at the prospect of memorizing even three names at one time, calm down. There are tricks for committing names to your short-term memory. If you have personally invited the guests to your hostess's group showing, you can memorize their names ahead of time. Then, at the showing, you will only need to attach the names you already know to the faces you are meeting.

To memorize someone's name whom you are meeting for the first time, make a point of immediately saying her name three times. "Esther, it is so nice to meet you. Esther, how long have you known our hostess?" or "Esther, I think our hostess is having everyone place their coats in the first room to your right down the hallway."

Another trick for memorizing someone's name is to associate it with something that is familiar or easy to remember. For example, when you meet someone whose name is the same as a friend of yours, picture your friend as you look at your new acquaintance. If your hostess's best friend is Betty, think "b.b.b." for Betty's her best buddy. Names can be associated in numerous ways, and can include references such as: bib-lical names; geographical locations; television, book, and movie charac-ters; and inanimate objects. You might associate the name Anne with "Annie Oakley" or "Anne of Green Gables." Cindy might be remem-bered as Cinnamon because she has auburn hair. Tammy might be associated with *The Taming of the Shrew*. It doesn't really matter, as long as the association helps you remember the name...and as long as you do not call someone by your word association instead of her name!

I have also found that giving each guest a "wish list" in the beginning of the evening gives me another opportunity to make certain I can address everyone by their first names. As I greet each guest, I provide her with a blank sheet of paper entitled "Wish List." I tell her to use her "wish list" throughout my presentation to jot down notes, questions, or products she would like. On top of her "wish list," using a thick black felt pen, I write her name in large bold black letters. In this way I can sneak a peek at her list should I forget her name.

TWELVE STEPS TO A SUCCESSFUL
GROUP DEMONSTRATION

Step #1—Thank-You and Welcoming

"The first thing I would like to do is thank our hostess, Susanne, for allowing me to come into her home and introduce all of you to Camelion's sheer non-run hosiery and our brand new sterling silver jewelry line. I would also like to extend a warm welcome to all of the guests here tonight. The thing I enjoy the very most in my business is meeting so many different and special people. I am truly happy to be here tonight."

Step #2—Tell What the Hostess Will Earn

"As my thank-you for having me in her home, I have brought along a small gift for Susanne. Susanne will also have an opportunity to earn fifty dollars worth of free products when two of you book showings of your own and when the group sales are over two hundred dollars. Susanne has preselected her gift and has chosen a Gold Scroll necklace and matching bracelet."

Note: Stating what your hostess can earn is not being "pushy" or "ag-gressive"; rather, it is a way of letting everyone know that you appreciate your hostess. The guests want their hostess to earn a gift and would think you were not very appreciative if you did not reward her efforts.

Notice, too, that I recommend providing a small gift of appreciation which is presented to the hostess at the beginning of the show. This gift can be totally unrelated to your business, and can include items such as note paper, flowers, decorative soap, a potpourri, etc. Make certain the gift is tastefully wrapped and presented with a smile and a thank-you!

Step #3—Outline the Presentation to Come

"Tonight I am going to give you a brief history of our company and tell you a bit about our wonderful business opportunity. Next, I will show you our product lines. I will teach you how to use hosiery as an accessory as well as what shapes of earrings and lengths of necklaces each of you should wear to enhance your unique face shapes and neck lengths. I will need our hostess and some volunteers for that portion of my class. Of course, we will have a question and answer period. At the end of my presentation, which will take approximately forty-five minutes, I would like to meet with each of you individually to answer any personal questions you might have. Susanne will be serving refreshments at that point too."

Step #4—A Brief Company History

Clients are curious and will appreciate a bit of background on the company from which you obtain your wholesale goods.

"Camelion was founded in 1984. Frustrated by hosiery that ran, didn't fit, and was uncomfortable, Joy Ross, our company president, wanted to offer women the hosiery she had always wanted. Hence, Camelion sheer non-run hosiery was developed. In 1988, Camelion's line expanded to include Italian sterling silver jewelry."

Step #5—Team-Building Talk

Your top-notch team-building talk should: tell your audience why you started your own direct sales business, stress your belief in your products and your company, and include the benefits of being in business for yourself such as controlling your time, setting your own income level, and tax advantages. As well, your team-building talk should inform the group of the high earning potential, that training and support is pro-vided, and that a direct sales business can be conducted on a part- or full-time basis. Your talk should be tailored in such a way that your particular audience can relate to the fact that a direct sales business would enhance their lives. For instance, if there are young moms in the group, talk about the advantages of being able to schedule your business around your family. If there are career women in the audience, stress your company's management opportunities.

"I started wearing Camelion hosiery about six months ago and I was extremely impressed with their comfort, fit, and durability. When my consultant asked me if I would be interested in marketing Camelion products, my first thought was, why not? Here was my opportunity to help other women alleviate their hosiery frustrations. Of course, as you know, Camelion now offers a wonderful sterling silver jewelry line. Our jewelry was introduced with the same foresight as our non-run hosiery. The company recognized that most women in North America had been color analyzed and that the majority were 'blue-skin-toned winters and summers.' With this in mind, and knowing that 'winters' and 'summers' should wear clothing and accessories with 'blue tones,' the company knew that silver would be this decade's jewelry craze. Aren't they smart?

"My dealings with the company have been nothing short of wonderful. Everyone at the head office is helpful and pleasant. It is interesting to note that the directors at the head office and many of the managers in the field own shares in our company.

"Having told you why I chose to market Camelion products, I would like to tell you that I also have a full-time job as a legal secretary. I dedicate one to two nights per week to my Camelion business. Over the past six months my business has taken me to Hawaii, purchased a new entertainment center for my apartment, and started a savings account for a down payment on a condominium. I have accomplished all of this with only part-time work! I have also established over 150 happy clients. When I have 300 clients, I intend to quit my secretarial job and conduct my Camelion business full-time. I have always believed that the only employer who will pay you what you are worth is you!

"Watch me tonight and ask yourself if a part- or full-time career with Camelion might be the answer to your dreams and aspirations. So far, I have helped five ladies to start their own Camelion businesses and I am now a manager. Each of my team members enjoys: tax deductions not normally allowed salaried individuals, the freedom to choose her own hours of work, and the ability to set her own income level.

"Everyone in Camelion has the opportunity to promote herself to management, just as I did. If you have ever been stuck in a dead-end job, you will appreciate the fact that in Camelion you promote yourself when you are ready. Whether you are looking for an additional source of income or an entirely new career, I strongly urge you to take a look at Camelion's business opportunity. Camelion has one of the highest profit structures in the industry and we have women and men from all different occupations and skill levels. We have social workers, home-makers, secretaries, nurses, accountants, and the list goes on. We also have many young moms who want to help with the family income yet still be home with their children throughout the day. By having their own businesses, they can schedule their appointments around their families.

"My Camelion business is a lot of fun and keeps my life interesting and varied. I have left a couple of pamphlets covering Camelion's business opportunity on the coffee table. Feel free to take one home with you. And, feel free to ask me for more information when we meet individually after my presentation."

Note: Whether or not you intend to enter management, you will discover many benefits in building a direct sales team of your own. In addition to receiving higher discounts, bonuses, or commissions from your direct marketing company, you will reap the rewards of helping others and polishing your own sales skills. There is no better training tool for an independent consultant than teaching someone else the ropes. The more you know about your business, the more profit you will enjoy. Make a practice of looking for one new team member at every group demonstration you conduct. In this way, over time, with a mini-mal amount of effort, you will build a nice-sized team.

Step #6—The Demonstration

The demonstration portion of your group showing is very similar to your individual presentation. The only difference is that, instead of talking with one person, you are talking to a group. As such, your group presentation should incorporate all of the varied needs that you have heard identified by individuals you have serviced.

Where possible, your group demonstration should encourage par-ticipation from the audience. For instance, when you are outlining the benefits and features of your products, ask if anyone in the group identifies with what you are saying. When conducting Camelion socials I often ask the guests if they have ever had an embarrassing run spoil the look of their outfit. Needless to say, every woman nods her head. Following this question, I kiddingly ask one of the guests how many people drew attention to the fact that she had a run in her hosiery. Make a point of ensuring that each guest at your group showing participates in your demonstration at least once. Involving the guests in your presentation makes them feel special and builds rapport.

Most likely your company provides a flip chart or agenda for you to follow when you are conducting group showings. Study it forward and backward. Your company's recommended presentation was compiled by experts and has been handed to you on a silver platter. Don't try to rewrite the script; it has already been perfected. Instead, conduct your company's recommended presentation professionally and confidently.

Step #7—The Question and Answer Period

Although the guests have probably been asking questions throughout your presentation, I recommend that you make an official request for questions before you do your group close. In this way, if you have forgotten to cover an important point, someone in the group will raise it as a question. Asking if there are any questions also lets your audience know that you are concerned that they have all the information they need to make their decision to purchase your products.

Consultant: "Before I complete my presentation, does anyone have any questions?"

When answering a question, always repeat the question to make certain you understand what is being asked. Then, completely answer the question before you move forward to another point. As well, always check to make certain that the person who asked you the question understands and is satisfied with your answer.

Guest: "Would you please explain your company's guarantee again?"

Consultant: "I would love to. Is there a particular part of our guarantee that you would like me to go over?"

Guest: "Well, what I am really wondering is how long your guarantee lasts. What if I decide I am not happy with my purchase after I have used it for three months?"

Consultant: "You want to know if I would honor our guarantee after you had been using our products for awhile. My answer is yes. Our

company guarantee does not have a time limit. If you feel you are satisfied with your purchase, then we are pleased. If you are not satisfied,
in any way, then you can exchange your products or have your full purchase price refunded. In our company, the client is always right. Does
that answer your question?"

Guest: "Basically, but what if you quit your business?"

Consultant: "You are wondering how you would ensure that your
guarantee was honored if I were to move or quit my business. Well, I do
not anticipate quitting my business or moving; however, if I were no
longer able to service you, I would make certain that another consultant
or my manager took care of you. You could also contact the company
directly to have your guarantee honored if I were no longer available to
service you. Does that alleviate your concern?"

Guest: "Yes. Thank you."

Step #8—Your Group Close

Your group close should:

1) Reinforce your company guarantee and why you think everyone
should be using your products and services,

2) Remind your guests that you would like to meet with everyone
individually,

3) Suggest that if anyone has to leave early, that she meet with you
first,

4) State what you recommend your new clients purchase as well as
outline what *most* of your clients purchase (as a general rule, people will
do whatever they feel is normally done; therefore, when you tell the
guests that *most* of your clients purchase a particular set of goods, or take
advantage of savings available in a particular value package, they will
too!),

5) Outline any company policies such as asking your clients not to
share value packages or share product systems which are designed to
work together,

6) Remind the guests that your hostess will now be serving refreshments,

7) Inform the guests as to when you will deliver any products they
order, and

8) Unlike the individual presentation, incorporate the cost of your
products or services.

"Our hostess will be serving refreshments in just a moment. I hope everyone enjoyed themselves today. Now, before I hand out order forms, I would like to remind you of Camelion's guarantee of total client satisfaction and explain our hosiery value packages. A four- to six-month supply of six pairs of hosiery is $31.80. When you take an eight-month to one-year supply of twelve pairs of hosiery they are $57.60. Although Camelion hosiery is available at $5.95 per pair, most of my clients choose to take advantage of the savings and convenience of shopping in bulk. I truly hope each of you takes a selection of hosiery home with you today, because I personally believe every woman should wear hosiery that lasts, saves her money, and gives her the security of never having to worry about a nasty run spoiling the look of her outfit. I also want to tell you that our company asks that you do not share value packages.

"You will find the value of our sterling silver jewelry outlined in our Client Brochures on the coffee table. Please feel free to take one. You will notice that we have something for everyone's shopping needs. As I mentioned earlier, our sterling silver jewelry is valued according to weight and many pieces are under ten dollars.

"In case you are wondering how long it will take for me to deliver the products you order, I want you to know that I have everything with me today.

"I am going to be taking a short break and then, I would like to meet with each of you individually. If anyone must leave early, I suggest that you meet with me first. Thank you for listening to me today, and I hope I can be of service to each of you."

Step #9—Your Individual Trial Close

Once you have taken a break, ask the guest who said she must leave early to meet with you.

"Phyllis, I know you have to leave early, so why don't you come and meet with me now?"

Once you and your client are seated, ask for the sale in the same manner that you would if you had just conducted an individual sales presentation. Study the following examples.

"Phyllis, why don't I help you select your hosiery shades first, and then we can talk about what sterling silver jewelry you would like to take home with you?"

"Jolee, would you like to begin by selecting your favorite sterling silver jewelry pieces or hosiery shades?"

"Charlotte, I hope you enjoyed yourself tonight. I know I did. What have you decided to take home with you tonight?"

"Lorelei, have you decided to take advantage of our hosiery value package of six or twelve pairs?"

Step #10—Answer Questions, Close, and Write Up Order

Client: "I would like to take everything home tonight. Your sterling silver is beautiful and I love your hosiery. Unfortunately, I am afraid that I can only afford to spend about twenty dollars."

Consultant: "Don't worry, together we will ensure you eventually own every piece of silver and every color of hosiery that you desire. Why don't we start by selecting a few hosiery shades for you? Which color of hosiery do you wear the most often?"

Client: "Beige."

Consultant: "Well then, let's order you two pairs of beige hosiery to start. What other colors do you like?"

Client: "I like the taupe, black, smoke grey and charcoal."

Consultant: "Jolee, I know you said that you can only afford to spend $20 tonight. Four pairs of hosiery at $5.95 is $23.80, and six pairs is only $31.80. For an additional $8, you can take home two extra pairs. Is there any reason why you couldn't take home all six pairs and take advantage of the savings?"

Client: "No, I suppose I could take six pairs."

Consultant: "Great! Jolee, would you please write your full name, address, and phone number on the top portion of this receipt?"

Step #11—Book More Showings

Using your technique for booking group demonstrations from group demonstrations, book a minimum of two of the guests to hold showings of their own. Remember to establish the date each booking is to be held. A booking that is not attached to a date is not a true booking.

Consultant: "Jolee, I know you are going to love your Camelion hosiery. I will phone in about two days to make certain that you truly love the luxury of wearing non-run hosiery. Earlier you mentioned that you wished you could take everything home with you tonight, which leads me to the following suggestion. At each group showing that I hold I always select one or two people that I would most like to have as my future hostesses. Even before you mentioned that you could only spend twenty dollars tonight, I was thinking that I would really enjoy having you as a hostess. You seem very nice and everyone admires you; and as a hostess, you can earn fifty dollars in free products! Is there any reason why you couldn't have a few friends over and hostess a showing of your own? I know you would be a terrific hostess!"

Client: "I would love to be a hostess, but everyone I know is here tonight."

Consultant: "You must have had a nice time seeing everyone you know. Don't worry about the fact that all your friends were here today. I am certain that most of them weren't able to pick up everything they wanted today and would appreciate another opportunity to view Camelion's selection of jewelry and hosiery. And, if you like, we could ask your friends to bring someone with them who wasn't here today."

Client: "I suppose so. But we will have to book my showing for a few weeks down the road or my friends won't have any money to spend."

Consultant: "That is a great idea. Which would be better for you, two or three weeks from now?"

Client: "Three weeks from now would be better."

Consultant: "Then we will book your showing for the week of the twenty-fifth. Would you prefer to have an evening or daytime class; and would you like to have your class at the beginning or the end of the week?"

Client: "I would prefer an evening class near the beginning of the week."

Consultant: "Tuesday or Wednesday evening?"

Client: "Wednesday."

Consultant: "Wednesday night it is then. Would you like to start at 7:30 or 8:00?"

Client: "Eight o'clock would be great."

Step #12—Start Coaching Your New Hostess

Begin coaching this new hostess and arrange a time the next day when you can call her to explain the steps involved in successful group showings.

Consultant: "Jolee, I am really looking forward to doing your show on Wednesday, the twenty-seventh at 8:00. I would like you to do a small favor for me. Would you please make certain that you mark our special date on your family calendar? I would feel awful if you double booked us by mistake and your family will appreciate knowing which night you are having guests."

Hostess: "I will do that as soon as I get home."

Consultant: "Great. Jolee, there are a few other points I would like to go over with you; however, our time is limited tonight. Is there a time tomorrow that would be convenient for me to call you and chat for a few minutes?"

Hostess: "After dinner would be great. Why don't you call me about 7:00?"

Consultant: "I will do that."

ENSURING THAT YOUR GROUP SHOWINGS ARE SUCCESSFUL!

Tip #1—Be Prepared

We have already talked about the importance of studying your company flip chart or suggested group demonstration presentation. If you are a new consultant, I suggest that you study your flip chart two or three times; then, after you are completely familiar with the contents, highlight one or two key words in each segment. You will want to present your products professionally and confidently, yet you want to talk from the heart...not read from your flip chart.

Be certain to take the following with you to your group demonstration.

1) Your datebook for scheduling future bookings.

2) Your hostess thank-you gift.

3) Your display, flip chart, demonstration aids, and inventory if you are offering your clients on-the-spot delivery.

4) Pens or pencils for your clients to use to take notes.

5) "Wish lists" for all of the guests.

6) A cashbox for making change.

7) A receipt book.

8) A calculator.

9) Business cards.

10) Team-building literature.

11) Client brochures.

12) A great attitude and a big smile.

Tip #2—Leave Your Problems at the Doorstep!

Undoubtedly, there will be times when you would rather not be conducting a group demonstration, but would rather be home with your family or out with friends. Occasionally, you may even be feeling a little under the weather before a group showing. Regardless, you must act enthusiastic and professional. Chances are that once you have started your presentation, you will begin to feel excited and energetic. You will definitely feel happy when you leave the group demonstration with new clients, two bookings, and substantial profits in your pocket!

Tip #3—Start with Small Groups

New consultants who are nervous should limit the number of guests at their first showing to three or four people. Then, with each showing you hold, increase the number of guests by one or two people. In no time at all, you will feel quite confident and capable.

Tip #4—Focus on Your Audience

I stopped being nervous about talking to large groups of people when I decided to stop worrying if they liked me. Once I changed my emphasis to ensuring my audience was having a great time, I felt relaxed. Whether or not I made a mistake, or forgot to say something, no longer mattered. What did matter was that my clients received the information I promised to deliver when I originally booked the group demonstration!

Tip #5—Be on Your Best Behavior

When conducting an individual or group sales presentation, the following rules of etiquette apply.

Arrive on time.

Never swear or tell off-color jokes.

Avoid religious and political discussions.

Never make racial or ethnic slurs.

Don't smoke, even if your hostess or client does. (If you are dying to have a cigarette, sneak out to your car during the break after your group close.)

Don't chew gum.

Although it is quite acceptable to have a few refreshments, don't eat more than your share.

Don't wear out your welcome; leave as soon as you have presented your hostess with the total group sales and any gifts she has earned.

At the end of the evening, formally thank your hostess for having you in her home.

CHAPTER SUMMARY

• Through probing and active listening, the role of the salesperson is to determine her clients' needs and wants, and then to educate her clients as to how the benefits and features of her products and/or services can satisfy them.

• Consumers want educated, honest, friendly businesspeople to market products they need and want directly to them in the comfort of their homes or offices.

• The ten steps for an effective sales presentation are:
1) Set the tone
2) Your opening remarks
3) Probing
4) Your presentation
5) Your trial close
6) Answer questions professionally
7) Your second close
8) Write up the order
9) Ask for referrals
10) Thank your client and reinforce her purchase

• Although somewhat less personal, your group demonstration should incorporate the same principles as your individual presentation and should include:
1) A thank-you to your hostess and a warm welcome to guests
2) Prizes the hostess can earn
3) An outline of the presentation to come
4) A brief company history
5) A top-notch team-building talk
6) A demonstration of the benefits and features of your products and services

  7) A question and answer period

  8) A group close

  9) An individual close with each guest

• Your top-notch team-building talk should: tell your audience why you started your own business, stress your belief in your products and your company, and include the benefits of being in business for yourself.

• Where possible, your group demonstration should encourage participation from the audience.

• When answering a question, always repeat the question to make certain you understand what is being asked. Then, completely answer the question before moving forward to another point.

• To ensure your group showings are successful:

  1) Be prepared

  2) Be sure that you have the necessary business supplies

  3) Leave your problems at the doorstep

  4) Start with small groups if you are nervous

  5) Be on your best behavior

DIARY TO SUCCESS

CHAPTER SEVEN

Skyrocketing Profits through Client Service

With the majority of sales in North America being repeat business, it is a wise businessperson who keeps her promise of follow-up service. Unfortunately, fearing rejection from dissatisfied clients, many consultants fail to service their clients and avoid reorder calls. Do not make this mistake!

No one likes to be criticized or enjoys hearing negative comments about the products she markets. Yet, it is a fact of business that some of your clients will be dissatisfied with their initial purchases and will require further servicing before they will change their opinions. It is true, too, that you will not be able to satisfy the needs of a small minority of clients and will be faced with refunding their purchase price, thereby losing the profit portion of your sale. (Most direct sales companies offer a company-backed client guarantee of total satisfaction, so you will not likely lose money on the wholesale cost of goods returned by clients.)

On a brighter note, the majority of your clients will be happy with their purchases and most of the feedback you receive will be positive. Unfortunately, too often it is the negative feedback that stands out in a new consultant's mind and causes her to question the quality of her products and services. In all aspects of life, criticism speaks louder than compliments, so this is not a surprising phenomenon. When someone we respect lists numerous positive traits about us and one tiny piece of disapproval, for hours the point we ponder over is the criticism. Simply stated, the reason for this is our need for approval, love, and acceptance. Therefore, a fear of client disapproval is quite natural; however, it is also unnecessary. In fact, you should welcome negative feedback from clients with enthusiasm.

Why on earth should you be enthused by expressed client dissatisfaction? Because you have a chance to change the situation and turn your unhappy client into a happy client who will order from you for years to come. Think for a moment. If you do not know your client is dissatisfied, you cannot correct the situation, and instead, you will be left wondering why she has not reordered. Be aware too that a dissatisfied client will tell all of her friends how she feels about the products you market. "Bad news" spreads much quicker and farther than "good news"!

With a little effort, patience, and good communication skills, discontented clients can be turned into satisfied customers. The majority of dissatisfied clients will be satisfied through an exchange of products or additional servicing; only a few will request that their full purchase price be refunded. Even those who ask to have their money returned will be pleased that you honored your guarantee of client satisfaction.

Make a promise to yourself to welcome feedback from your clients...be it good or bad. Also make a commitment to yourself, your business, and your clients to ensure that every customer is a satisfied customer. Remember, you are building a business, and the "easy" money is attained through reorders. Securing a reorder requires far less effort than: prospecting for and locating a new client, establishing a relationship of mutual trust and respect with your client, conducting a full product demonstration, and cementing the close.

KNOW THE POTENTIAL PROBLEMS
YOUR CLIENTS MIGHT ENCOUNTER

Be prepared for whatever feedback you may receive when you are servicing clients. To do this you will need to be totally familiar with your products. What are the potential problems a client may encounter when she uses your products or services? What are the solutions to these potential problems? In Camelion, inexperienced consultants sometimes place a new client in the wrong size of hosiery. If the hosiery are too large, the client will find that her pantyhose will bag and sag. The opposite may also be true, and the client may find that the hosiery split in the panty portion because they are too small. Knowing this in advance helps our Camelion consultants to service their clients confidently. Therefore, part of our new consultant training program includes instructions on how to fit clients properly, as well as potential problems which indicate a client has been improperly fitted.

If you are not aware of the potential problems of your particular products, contact your manager or company and ask for more information.

Remember, you are not in business by yourself. Your manager, fellow consultants, and company want to be sure you succeed and will help you in every way possible. I guarantee that your manager and company will have a solution to any problem you encounter in your business.

Should the situation arise where you are servicing a client with a complaint for which you do not have a solution or explanation readily available, simply tell your client that: 1) you are pleased that she has brought her concerns to your attention, 2) that you will consult your manager or company regarding a solution, and 3) that within forty-eight hours you will recontact your client with an answer to her problem or to arrange for a full refund.

In a situation where you contact a client and find she simply does not like your products, do not panic. First, try to establish why your client is dissatisfied. Next, offer solutions to the problems she is experiencing. If your client insists she will never be satisfied, offer to exchange her products or refund her purchase price. Obviously, it is far more advantageous for you to exchange products, thereby securing the profit portion of your sale, while recouping the wholesale cost of the returned goods through a product exchange with your company. However, never argue with a customer who insists on having her money refunded.

WILL SOME CLIENTS TAKE ADVANTAGE OF MY GUARANTEE?

Yes, some people will take advantage of your guarantee policy. I can remember one Camelion client who purchased six pairs of hosiery, and after wearing her pantyhose for three months, asked for an exchange on the basis that she was not satisfied with the length of wear she had received. On examination of her hosiery, I discovered that they were still in good condition and she would probably get another month to three months wear from her initial six pairs. However, because in Camelion the client is always right, I honored our guarantee. Three months later, she requested another exchange. Again, there was no need for her to request an exchange. My solution was to say to my client, "Perhaps you will never be satisfied with Camelion hosiery. Why don't I refund your full purchase price so that you can resume purchasing your previous brand of hosiery?" You guessed it. She wasn't interested in going back to wearing her previous hosiery brand, and wanted to continue buying Camelion. I am happy to report that she never asked to have the guarantee honored again and is still happily wearing Camelion hosiery.

Having a company guarantee of total client satisfaction does not mean that you should permit clients to abuse your guarantee. Should you experience a similar situation to the one I have outlined above, it may be in your best interest to offer to refund your client's purchase price. Most often, clients who inappropriately ask you to honor your company's guarantee will be satisfied with an explanation as to what they can and cannot expect from your products. The majority of customers are honest and will not abuse your guarantee, so learn to take those that do in stride. The numerous types of personalities you will encounter throughout your business career will help to keep your life varied and interesting. Don't let one or two dishonest clients spoil your fun!

YOU ARE BUILDING A BUSINESS REPUTATION!

The number one complaint of direct sales clients is their inability to locate businesspeople to service their faulty products and reorders. Too often, direct sales clients find they have been promised prompt, professional service only to discover that after the initial sale, they never hear from their consultant again. As we explored earlier, fear of rejection and disapproval are the main reasons why some businesspeople fail to service their clients. Unfortunately, another reason for poor client service is that some consultants quit their businesses and simply abandon their established clientele. This is a highly unfair situation that should never arise.

If you decide to close your business, or take an extended leave of absence, your future business reputation depends on you turning your list of clients over to someone who will continue to service them. When you ensure that your clientele continues to be properly serviced, they will remain loyal to you should you have future business or personal dealings with them. On the other hand, if you totally abandon your clients, you will never re-establish their loyalty. Therefore, should you decide to close your business, contact your manager or company and ask them to give you the name of a consultant who will ensure your clients are properly serviced.

KEEPING CLIENT RECORDS

In order to service your clients properly, you will need to maintain accurate records of their purchases and the dates you should contact them for reorders. To accomplish this you will need two files—an alphabetical file of your clients' names, addresses, phone numbers, and purchases; and a separate chronological file denoting your clients' names and filed according to the month in which you are to service them again.

Alphabetical Files

Your alphabetical files can also be used to keep personal notes about your clients. For instance, you may want to keep records of your clients' birthdays, their family members' birthdays, their favorite hobbies, vacations they may be planning, courses they are taking, etc. In this way, you can comment on matters of personal significance to your clients when you are conducting your servicing calls. Everyone wants to feel special and the fact that you have made the effort to take notes on their personal activities and special occasions will leave a favorable lasting impression with your clients. You can also use the information in your alphabetical files to obtain additional sales for birthday and anniversary gifts.

Sample Alphabetical File Card

Front:

PARKS, CAROLINE	Cindy Smith's party—09/06/90	
Client's name	How and when met client	
Home: 555-5555	Work: 222-2222	
Phone numbers		
111 A Street,	Seattle, WA	00000
Street address	City State/Province	Zip code
01/12/56 02/14	Jack, 11/17/54	
Birthday Anniversary	Husband's name & birthday	
David, 11/10/80 Brian, 04/17/82		
Children's names and birthdays		

ADDITIONAL NOTES

Hobbies: Writing, swimming, and camping.

Occupation: Is a self-employed bookkeeper.

Vacation: Is planning to tour France by bike this summer.

Back:

PARKS, CAROLINE
Client's name

DATE OF PURCHASE	WHAT PURCHASED
10/04/90	Complete skin care line for oily skin
11/06/90	Skin freshener and black mascara

Chronological Files

The purpose of your chronological files is to remind you when you are to service your clients. Your clients should be serviced within one week of making their initial purchases and every two months thereafter. Regardless of whether or not your clients need additional products every two months, recontacting them on a regular basis will keep your name and products fresh in their minds.

Note: When you are servicing your clients, make a point of asking for referrals. You may even want to offer an incentive gift to ensure you receive numerous leads for prospective clients. For instance, you may want to conduct a monthly drawing for a special prize for everyone who gives you a referral, or offer your clients a percentage off their next purchases when someone they recommend becomes a customer. The cost of the incentive gift you offer for referrals should not exceed 10 percent of the profit you anticipate will be generated.

SPECIAL MAILINGS

Some businesspeople find it extremely beneficial to send birthday, Christmas and anniversary cards to their clients. For a few dollars and a bit of extra effort and time, your clients will be reminded of the fact that you care about them. Everyone loves to be remembered on special occasions. Why not let your clients know they are appreciated?

Another good mailing technique is to send out quarterly client newsletters. Modern technology has made access to professionally drafted newsletters affordable and easy. Why not keep your clients informed of current changes in your field? If you are marketing fashion-related products (clothing, skin care, makeup, jewelry, or hosiery), you may find it useful to prepare and distribute quarterly or biannual fashion updates to your clients. Your clients will also appreciate knowing about improved and additional products and services you are offering. When you are having a sale to clear out last season's items, announce your promotion in a colorful one-page brochure. Have you attained a targeted sales goal or a new level with your company? Send your clients a letter telling them that you appreciate their support in helping you to achieve your desires and dreams. Everyone wants to be associated with a winner and to feel they have been a part of someone else's success!

HOLD AN OPEN HOUSE FOR YOUR CLIENTS

A great way to service all of your clients, especially when you are introducing new products or conducting a clearance sale, is to hostess your own open house. To be certain that your open house is a great success, prepare official invitations and mail them to your clients two or three weeks in advance. Then, three or four days before your showing, follow up by phone and remind everyone to attend.

When inviting clients to come, present your open house as the most exciting "must attend" event of the season. Tell your customers that you are looking forward to seeing them and that you are thrilled that they will be visiting you in your home. Remember, in order to ensure a great turnout, you must make certain that your clients feel they will benefit from attending your open house!

Note: To avoid investing too much time in your open house, I recommend confining your showing to three or four hours on one particular day or evening.

Sample Invitation

CAROLINE PARKS

As a valued client and friend you are invited to attend a preview of this season's rainbow of cool and warm toned blushers, eye shadows, and lip shades. This special event will be held at my home on

Saturday, September 5, 1990 at 99 B Street, Vancouver, B.C. between 1:00 P.M. and 4:00 P.M.

Refreshments will be served. An early bird drawing for a bottle of our tantalizing new "Evening Whisper" perfume will be held at 2:00 P.M. Bring a friend with you and receive a 10 percent discount!

R.S.V.P. by telephone
Louise Dennison
Independent Consultant
The Beauty of You Cosmetics
(604) 555-5555

OFFER GIFT WRAPPING

During holiday seasons, everyone is busy and pressed for time. Help make your clients' shopping obligations easier by offering to wrap items purchased as gifts.

Every time you contact your clients, remind them about your gift wrapping service and ask if they are celebrating any special occasions in the near future. Stress the fact that your guarantee of total client satisfaction combined with your personal service ensures that a gift chosen from your product line will be the perfect gift!

Note: Holidays such as Christmas, Easter, Mother's Day, Father's Day, and Valentine's Day provide you with increased opportunities for sales. Prepare for these occasions all year long. For example, when one of your clients "falls in love" with an item she simply can't afford, ask her if she would like you to contact her husband or children prior to the next special occasion she is celebrating and suggest they purchase the item as a gift for her.

CLIENT SERVICE...A PROGRAM FOR PROFIT!

Earlier I stated that the "easy money" is obtained through reorders. Study the following chart to see why you should provide continual, professional, prompt service to each of your clients.

Possible Annual Purchase Per Client	Time Worked Per Sale
Initial purchase $100	One hour
First reorder ....$ 50	Half-hour
Second reorder ....$ 30	Fifteen minutes
Open house purchase ....$ 25	Fifteen minutes

Birthday gift purchase .... $ 25   Half-hour

Christmas gift purchases .... $100   One hour

Valentine's Day purchase .... $ 15   Half-hour

Easter purchase .... $ 15   Half-hour

Total purchases per year: Total hours worked:

$360   4 1/2 hours

Now, divide $360 in half to attain your gross profit of $180. Next, divide $180 by 4 1/2 hours to attain your pay rate of $40 per hour.

As you can see, even when you begin your business on a part-time basis, direct marketing can be extremely profitable. Let's take a more detailed look at your potential part-time income.

Conducting just two group demonstrations per week will easily result in ten new clients per week. Ten new clients multiplied by fifty weeks equals 500 new clients in your first year of business. Five hundred clients times an average annual gross profit per client of $180 results in a possible $90,000 profit for your second year of business, with forty hours per week dedicated toward your business. Wow! Even if you divide this figure in half to allow for clients moving or changing brand loyalties, you still have the potential for a second-year business gross profit of $45,000. As you can see, properly servicing your clients can result in substantial profits!

There is only one person who can ensure that you will enjoy the level of profits outlined above...you! Only you can study and learn all there is to know about your products. Only you can practice and use the techniques for success outlined in this book and in your company training manual. Only you can service your clients with the individual care and attention they deserve. You are the only one who can secure your place at the top. Make today the day you start building your financial future!

CHAPTER SUMMARY

• With the majority of sales in North America being repeat business, it is a wise businessperson who keeps her promise of follow-up service.

• The majority of your clients will be happy with their purchases, and with a little effort, patience, and good communication skills, discontented clients can be turned into satisfied clients.

• When servicing clients, you should be prepared for whatever feedback you may receive, and know the solutions to potential problems which may arise.

• In order to service your clients properly, you will need to maintain accurate records of their purchases and the dates you should contact them for reorders.

• Great ideas for cementing your relationship with each of your clients include: sending special-occasion cards and quarterly newsletters, holding open houses, and offering a gift wrapping service.

• You are the only person who can ensure that you will enjoy the substantial profits generated by properly servicing your clients.

DIARY TO SUCCESS

CHAPTER EIGHT

Strategies for Increased Confidence and Profits

A positive self-image is crucial to health, happiness and success, yet self-love is a foreign concept to many. This is truly a sad reality that does not have to be. Everyone is worthwhile and important. Unfortunately, few of us recognize this truth, although we all seek its rewards.

Even as infants in our cribs we seek acceptance and love. Too tiny and dependent to care for ourselves, we look to our parents and siblings to comfort our ache to be loved. A baby who is denied love will die.

In grade school, we look to our teachers for praise. Very early we learn that our grades and athletic abilities often measure the degree of approval we experience. In high school we turn to our peers to determine our value. Throughout our dating years and marriage we often turn to the opposite sex to endorse our existence. Eventually, our children become measures of our importance. Finally, our financial and career achievements mirror our self-image of success. Wow! Where, when, and how do we learn to love ourselves for just being ourselves?

Because we are constantly striving to please and measure up to society's and our loved ones' expectations of what and who we should be, it is not surprising that we often do not stop to love and care for ourselves. The major problem with trying to live up to the expectations of others is that you will never be able to please everyone, and you will never be perfect at everything you tackle. In fact, a compulsive need for approval will cause you to feel less than adequate.

The root of a poor self-image starts when we are mere babes and our parents are forced to voice that ugly word, "No!" Too young to understand our need to be protected and guided, we feel that our wrongdoing means we are bad. Unfortunately, this feeling of being "bad" or "inadequate" may be reinforced numerous times throughout our schooling and dating years. Already emotionally battered, some people even choose life-mates who will continue a pattern of control through rewarding acceptable behavior and punishing unacceptable behavior.

As adults, we have the power to change our life patterns and take the steps necessary to begin feeling good about ourselves. No matter what your situation is today, you alone possess the power to maintain the status quo or move your life toward more happiness, satisfaction, and success. Furthermore, there are numerous sources of help to aid you on your way. Libraries, bookstores, adult education courses, support groups, churches, psychologists, and psychiatrists are excellent vehicles for information and support. At the back of this book I have recommended a few books that I feel are invaluable for self-love and growth. I recommend that you read one or more of these books, even if you do not believe you need them. No one can ever feel too good about herself, or too happy.

Why do I put such a great emphasis on self-worth? Because in order to be loved you must first love yourself. Because in order to succeed, you must first see yourself as deserving and being capable of success. Because in order to be happy you must first realize what you "need" to be happy. Because everyone, by virtue of their existence, has the right to be loved, successful, and happy!

Throughout my personal and business life, I have watched numerous people suffer in life situations that could be changed. Many individuals endure situations such as unhappy marriages, unsatisfactory jobs, poverty, loneliness, and illnesses that do not necessarily have to be. I believe that the vast majority of the misery I have seen could have been eliminated, yet it is mostly accepted as a way of life. Life is not preordained to be unhappy. Life is filled with opportunities to love and be loved. Opportunities to laugh, to sing, to feel warm and cared for are there for those who look for them. No one has to settle for less, unless she chooses to settle for less.

The only reason I can find to justify why so many people settle for less than their share of happiness in life is that they feel they are getting what they deserve. But almost everything one does in life is a choice. It is not that I believe that people who suffer choose to suffer; rather I believe they do not realize they have a choice. Recently I was talking with one of our consultants who is having marital difficulties. When I asked her why she continued in the relationship, she replied, "What choice do I have?" This woman is quite attractive and in her early fifties. Her children are grown, she has a good job and a part-time Camelion business. Obviously, she has many choices. From previous talks I have had with this woman, I know that her husband continually ridicules her physical form, intelligence, and worth. Being told on a daily basis that she is inadequate, it is not surprising that she has come to believe that the way her husband treats her is the way she deserves to be treated.

Our willingness to accept abuse is directly related to our need for approval and our inability to love ourselves. Certainly, had the lady mentioned above learned to love herself, she would never have married, never mind continued to live with, someone who obviously does not love himself or her.

Realizing that a feeling of self-worth is essential in order for one to have a happy life, it is a shame that we are not taught to love ourselves in school. I would dearly like to see our school curriculum contain courses on loving yourself and others. Instead, throughout society, self-love is ridiculed and scorned in statements such as: "Don't be so conceited," "Who do you think you are anyway?" "What did you expect?" "Children are meant to be seen and not heard," "A woman's place is in the home," "Don't be such a baby, men don't cry," and the list of falsehoods goes on.

Self-help books, psychologists, and psychiatrists would seem to be logical places for one to turn for help. Yet in society, people who seek professional help are often labelled as sick or weak. In view of the discrimination one must endure for seeking professional help, I would think that the opposite is true and that a person must be incredibly strong and sane to seek professional help. Personally, I would much rather trust the mental health of an individual who sought psychiatric help than one who denies its benefits and healing powers.

Unfortunately, it is a lack of belief in ourselves that often stops us from seeking the help we need. This is evident in statements such as: "What if I go to a shrink and find out that I am sick?" "What good would it do for me to find out what is wrong with my life? I can't do anything about it anyway!" "I can't afford the time or money required to indulge myself in such decadent treatment."

Regardless of whether or not you feel that professional help would benefit you, know one thing for certain…you must learn to trust, love, respect, and care for yourself before you can truly trust, love, respect, and care for others. In order to increase your self-esteem, you must nurture your personal value on a daily basis. Let's take a look at some self-depreciating attitudes that we can begin to correct on our own.

SELF-DEPRECIATING ATTITUDES	BUILDING ATTITUDES
I am a failure.	I am capable!
I can't do that because I might fail/people will laugh/it's too difficult.	I can do that because I want to and I believe I can!
I am not worthwhile.	I am worthwhile!
Someone won't let me do what I want to do.	I am in charge of my own destiny!
I must sacrifice for spouse/children/family	I am entitled to my own happiness!
Life is too difficult!	Life is difficult and challenging!
I am too tired to try.	Trying will give me the energy I need to succeed!
I am too old.	I am alive and healthy!
I am too young.	I am filled with the energy of youth!
I am uneducated.	I crave knowledge!
I am stupid.	I am capable of learning!
I am unattractive.	All human beings are beautiful!
I am too fat/skinny/ tall/short.	The inner self is where true beauty lies!
I do not have the money.	I am capable of getting as much money as I want!
I can't.	I can!

Knowing on which side of the above chart you operate most often will help you determine how little or how much self-worth you already possess. Learning to operate on the positive side more often simply requires a little energy and self-awareness.

The first step toward more self-confidence is becoming aware of how you perceive yourself. To do this I suggest you start with the above list, then continue adding your own positive and negative attitudes. Listen to your inner voice. What does your conscious mind tell you about you? Are the inner thoughts you feed yourself mostly positive or mostly negative? Next, ponder where these attitudes came from. Are they a true reflection of who you are, or is someone else negatively affecting your attitude toward yourself? What role are your parents still playing? What about your spouse? Is she/he helping to build your esteem...or destroy it? What do your friends tell you? Does everyone tell you the same thing, or do you get conflicting messages?

After completing the above exercise you may be surprised to discover that many of your self-depreciating attitudes are inaccurate. You will know they are inaccurate if you have been receiving conflicting messages from others. You will know your negative feelings of self-worth are incorrect if you do not really believe they are true or if they do not accurately reflect your accomplishments in life. And, because most people don't give themselves due credit, realize that any positive feelings you have about yourself are most likely to be true!

WHAT ABOUT MY NEGATIVE TRAITS?

Everyone has shortcomings that they wish they did not possess, and everybody makes mistakes. No one is perfect or totally self-confident. True self-confidence is the ability to accept and love yourself in spite of your faults.

Whenever you think of something you wish were different about yourself, ask yourself if you are capable of changing what you do not like. If you honestly can't or won't change what you dislike, then love yourself in spite of it. Should you decide you are capable of changing whatever it is you dislike, then develop a plan to do just that. Don't be too hard on yourself and don't try to change more than one major behavior or trait at a time. For instance, if you would like to lose ten pounds, then develop a plan to achieve your goal. However, if you would like to lose ten pounds and quit smoking, trying to accomplish both at one time will likely lead you to abandon both goals.

More importantly, make a point of concentrating on what you do like about yourself, instead of continually berating yourself for your shortcomings. By doing so, you will discover that you like more and more about yourself, and the things that you do not like will become less and

less important. Think for a moment. Who is more likely to lose unwanted weight—someone who loves herself or someone who continually chastises herself? Who is more likely to succeed in life...a person
with high self-esteem or someone with low self-esteem? The answers are
obvious, so start loving yourself for just being you!

NEVER COMPARE YOURSELF TO OTHERS

Comparing yourself to others will lead to self-destruction. There will
always be people who are more of what you would like to be, and there
will always be people who are less than you would like to be. When you
compare yourself to another, someone always loses...you or the other
guy. When you learn to accept yourself for who you are and to accept
others for who they are, everyone wins!

I sometimes hear consultants say such things as, "Of course she is
successful; her husband is a doctor," or "If I looked like her, I'd be
successful too!" My answer is always, "She has worked very hard to be
successful. Please don't diminish her accomplishments by attributing
them to something other than her willingness to be the best she can be."
Unfortunately, when we envy another person, we sometimes attribute
her success to good fortune rather than giving her due credit. The truth
is that good fortune accounts for a very small percentage of the success
people enjoy. Instead of feeling envious of others, investigate how they
became successful and then apply what you have learned. With the right
attitude and the acquisition of the necessary skills, you can achieve any
goal you set for yourself!

LEARN TO LOOK FOR THE GOOD
IN OTHERS

When you look for the good in others, you will find the good in you!
Gossip, swearing, criticism, racial slanders, and off-color jokes lower
your feelings of self-worth. You can't help but feel guilty when you break
a confidence with a friend, family member, or coworker. Even while you
are sharing the story with a third party, the little nagging voice inside of
you is saying, "You are wrong for not honoring the trust placed in you."
When you know that you are doing something that is wrong, you feel
bad about yourself. Break enough confidences and you will feel terrible.

People who often swear are demonstrating deep feelings of hurt and
anger. Happy, self-fulfilled people do not swear all of the time. I have a
girl friend whom I have known for over ten years. When I first met her,

she used to swear constantly. One day I asked her how swearing made her feel about herself. She looked puzzled and interested in what I had to say. I explained that although swearing was a great way to let the world know her dislikes and frustrations, I was certain it was doing damage to her. By continually doing something that made her feel bad inside, instead of ridding herself of unwanted negative thoughts, she was actually compounding the problem. Realizing how she was hurting herself, my friend stopped swearing.

Most individuals feel that swearing is wrong; therefore, when we swear, we feel bad about ourselves. If you are in a habit of swearing, stop and become aware of how your use of profane language is making you feel. Yes, you have a right to express your anger, hurt, and frustration; however, is swearing a healthy way for you to express what you feel? Wouldn't expressing your feelings clearly and openly help to heal your pain?

When you criticize others, you are really criticizing yourself. In fact, the more often I hear someone criticizing others, the more aware I become of how horrible she feels about herself. You have probably heard it said that the traits that we dislike most in others, reflect the traits which we dislike most in ourselves. I believe this is true. I used to work with a woman who was extremely critical of everyone else in the office. One day I asked her why she was so tough on everyone. She confessed that she worried about her own competence level and felt that if she could handle her job, surely everyone else should be better able to master theirs. This woman expected a lot from others because she saw them as being able to accomplish more than she could. After a lengthy discussion, the woman realized that the real problem was that she was a perfectionist and, as such, would never be able to meet her own ideals. She was not only too hard on others, she was too hard on herself!

People are people. Everyone has good days and bad days. No one is perfect and no one is on top of life all of the time. It is the differences between people that keeps life interesting. If everyone were exactly the same, all of the time, life would be boring. Learn to accept others for who they are and you will be better able to accept yourself. More importantly, learn to accept and love yourself, and you will be better able to accept and love others.

The proposition that when we criticize others, we are really criticizing ourselves, also applies to racial, ethnic, sexist, and denominational slurs and jokes. It is no more acceptable to allow others to make prejudiced remarks in our presence. There is only one mankind and the fact that we come from different countries, vary in color, practice different religions, and speak distinct languages is irrelevant to our worth as human beings. Everyone deserves to be on this planet and share in the same opportunities and life experiences as everyone else. No matter who you are, or what you have accomplished or believe, you do not have a right to judge the value of others. You may not be able to change the historical, economic, and political circumstances that are responsible for much of the discrimination we see today; however, you can control how you interpret and react to these occurrences.

Fear is at the root of most prejudiced remarks and jokes. For instance, the reason we tell sexist jokes is that we do not completely understand and trust the opposite sex. Laughing at and making fun of the things we fear lets us acknowledge our fear in an acceptable way. Unfortunately, although they make us laugh, off-color jokes have the negative effect of causing us to feel guilty, thereby lowering our self-esteem (not to mention the negative effect they have on others!).

Remember, learning to love yourself is the first step in learning to love others. When you discover the inherent value of mankind, yourself included, you will find happiness. Life is a gift and is far too short to spend fearing others and ourselves.

SUCCESS IS THE RESULT OF A POSITIVE ATTITUDE!

I would like you to think for a moment about an accomplished person whom you admire. What are the positive traits of this person? Write them down before you continue reading. List everything you can think of that leads you to admire the individual you have in mind. You may be surprised by what you see. Chances are your list includes some or all of the points listed below.

Intelligent/smart/educated/bright
Witty/funny/entertaining
Congenial/friendly/sociable
Dedicated/hardworking
Dependable/reliable
Caring/trustworthy/honest
Aware/well travelled/well read/informed
Attractive/well dressed

Intuitive
Rich/famous
Lucky

Which of the attributes listed above and on your list are learned and which ones are innate? In other words, how many of these traits does the person you admire come by because of birth, and how many has she mastered on her own? Let's take a closer look.

Although intelligence and attractiveness are to some degree the product of genes, everyone has a little of each. Some people are born rich or famous; however, in North America all of us have the opportunity to attain fame and fortune. For some of us the journey is longer, but we still have the opportunity. I do not believe one person has more luck than another; instead, I believe we make our own luck by taking advantage of the opportunities that come our way.

Every other trait on the list is learned. Being intuitive is simply a matter of listening to your heart and soul. All of us possess some degree of intuition. Being well dressed requires keeping updated on current fashion trends and paying attention to personal grooming. Being caring, trustworthy, and honest are learned behaviors. Becoming well travelled, aware, well read, and educated are all the result of personal choices. Being dependable, dedicated, reliable, and hardworking are acquired personality traits too! Anyone can learn to be congenial, friendly, sociable, witty, funny, and entertaining. The point is that most of the positive traits of accomplished individuals are mastered, not inborn. Therefore, we all possess, to varying degrees, the positive traits necessary for success.

Which of the positive traits of the person you listed above do you possess? I am willing to bet that you possess at least 80 percent. Now, with only 20 percent left to attain, why can't you be as accomplished as the person you admire most?

DRESS TO FEEL GOOD!

When I am lecturing on self-esteem, I love to ask the people in my audience to raise their hands if they totally love their bodies. Although this question always elicits much nervous laughter, to date, only two people have raised their hands in response to it. The vast majority of people wish they could change something about the way they look.

In a world where advertising is constantly pitching perfect images at us, it is difficult to live in the real world. Advertisers know that when they show a beautiful woman or man drinking a particular beverage, or driving a particular car, viewers will equate being beautiful with owning that car or drinking that beverage. Exploitive and sexist advertising must be effective because more and more products are being promoted in this way.

Exploitation and sexism in advertising is one of my pet peeves and I make a point of not purchasing products advertised in a manner that I find offensive. I wish everyone would do the same. I also wish everyone would write to the companies and advertising agencies in question and let them know that enough is enough! Promoters would have to listen if everyone wrote letters saying something such as, "Tell me what your product has to offer, don't just let me know that you can afford to hire beautiful models. I am an intelligent, feeling human being and I demand to be treated with respect. Give me credit for thinking, please!"

Very few people are happy about the way they look. Almost everyone wants to be taller or shorter, or heavier or lighter. Some people want a different nose; others straighter teeth. A few wish for smaller or bigger feet. This person wants to change the shape of the calves of her legs, and the other wants curlier hair. Some individuals wish they could change their whole body. Wow! How can someone be dissatisfied with a body that functions properly, keeps you free from pain, and takes you from one point to another? A body that encases your brain and soul and lets you feel and live should be worshipped, not ridiculed. The human body is a gift, no matter how tall or short it is. I agree that one should take care of one's body, but please don't ask it to be any more wonderful than it already is. It is your body...love it, nurture it, and keep it in good condition.

I once dated a man who continually hinted that I should lose ten pounds. Now, my body functions very well at its current height of five feet nine inches and weight of 145 pounds. I look and feel healthy, so I wondered why my ex-boyfriend was so concerned about ten pounds. One day I asked him if my losing ten pounds would in any way increase the quality of our relationship. He was stunned. He had to answer that it would not improve the quality of our association. Thank goodness, he never again mentioned my weight.

I do believe that if your health is affected by unwanted weight, you should work toward losing the extra pounds. I believe you should exercise three times per week, but for health reasons, not aesthetic reasons.

I also believe that you should strive to look your best, no matter what your physical state. Everyone feels better when they take proper care of their hair, teeth, skin, and body. The clothes you wear affect the way you feel too! I honestly believe you should only wear clothes that make you feel terrific, even if this means throwing away half of your wardrobe and spending money on yourself! You do not have to be rich to enjoy nice clothes. There are numerous secondhand stores with clothes at one-half to one-quarter of the original price. The reason these stores are popping up all over the place is that many people are looking for such items, so why shouldn't you?

When I started my direct selling career, I owned precisely one dress. It is fortunate that I felt terrific in this dress because I wore it constantly. I came to think of it as a uniform for success. Although it is worn thin from use, my black dress has become a keepsake because it reminds me of my road to success. How could I ever part with something that so often made me feel wonderful? So you see, you do not have to be rich to dress in a manner that makes you feel great. Over time, you can build a whole wardrobe of clothes that you love to wear.

If you have been planning to buy a new wardrobe once your current weight changes, stop and think for a moment. Wearing clothes that you do not like in hopes of one day buying new ones to suit a new body is self-defeating. You have to start loving yourself the way you are now, before you will be able to feel good enough about yourself to change your weight. Do yourself a favor and purchase a few new outfits now! Your new wardrobe will help to increase your self-esteem, which will aid you in your plan to change your weight.

It is true that first impressions create lasting impressions; therefore, when conducting business or stepping out socially, you should strive to look your best. Learn to behave and dress in ways that reflect your true inner self. Commit to being the best you can be today, and love and accept yourself for being you!

CONFIDENCE TRANSLATES INTO PROFITS

Recently, one of our managers, Annie, called to boast about her success at yet another group showing. Excitedly she told me that over the past month she had doubled her average show sales, from $200 to $400! I was excited too, and I asked her what changes she had made to increase her profits so dramatically.

"I'm good at what I do!" she replied enthusiastically. "Before, I was so self-conscious that I just read from my flip chart. Now, I'm more confident. I tell women these are the best pantyhose in the world and they have a right to own them. I've started dressing more professionally too. I bought myself a couple of new outfits that make me feel like a million dollars. I know that when my customers see me they know I am successful. And, I don't hesitate anymore. I just assume they will buy from me and they do!"

One of the most gratifying aspects of Annie's story is that less than six months before, during a management seminar, she confessed that she didn't feel very good about herself. She told the group that she wanted to lose fifteen pounds but found she couldn't. She also wanted to buy some new clothes but couldn't until she lost weight. Annie had put herself in a catch-22 situation. Every time she looked at herself in the mirror she was disappointed with what she saw because her clothes didn't fit properly and the unwanted weight was still there. With such a negative attitude it was no wonder she wasn't losing weight.

One of our company directors pointed out that by constantly dwelling on what she didn't like about herself, and by denying herself the new clothes she desired, she was destroying her self-esteem and making her goal to lose weight seem impossible. The director suggested that Annie start concentrating on what she did like about herself and, as an added boost, that she not wait until she lost her unwanted weight to buy a couple of new outfits. Obviously the director's advice was right on target because not only has Annie lost her first five pounds, but her increased self-confidence has also led to increased profits.

Annie's story is just one of many success stories that result when a consultant or manager starts to feel more confident. Throughout the years I have seen numerous, shy, self-conscious women (including myself) transform into prosperous, happy businesswomen. The key to success for every one of them was accepting themselves for who they were and learning to concentrate on their positive attributes. Remember, feeling good about yourself will free you from unnecessary self-doubt and give you the courage to concentrate on accomplishing your goals.

CHAPTER SUMMARY

• A positive self-image is crucial to health, happiness, and success.

• As adults, we have the power to change our life patterns and take the steps necessary to begin feeling good about ourselves.

- To increase your level of self-esteem, practice the following:

1) Read motivational and self-help books concerned with personal growth. Most of these books contain sections on self-esteem and confidence building. Read them often and take from them what you need to hear.

2) Start looking for what you like about yourself, and learn to love that which you do not like and cannot change.

3) Never compare yourself to others.

4) If your lack of confidence is extreme, seek professional help. Counselling is the most valuable gift you can give to yourself, your family, and your future.

5) Learn to look for the good in others and you will discover what is good about you. Gossip, criticism, swearing, racial slanders, and off-color jokes will lower your feelings of self-worth.

6) Make a point of looking your best at all times. Only wear clothes that make you feel like a million dollars. Feeling good about your personal appearance increases confidence.

7) Be kind to yourself. You are entitled to mistakes and successes. Don't berate yourself for your shortcomings; instead, praise yourself for being the best you can be today.

8) Confidence translates into profits!

9) Be open to change and work at one major self-improvement goal at a time. Rome was not built in a day.

DIARY TO SUCCESS

CHAPTER NINE

The Hidden Power of Goal Setting

The great majority of self-made millionaires began their journey by setting and mapping their plan to success. Goal setting has long been recognized as a powerful motivational and directional tool. Unfortunately, failing to see the value of or not being aware of the steps involved in successful goal setting, many people do not use this effective life and business practice.

WHAT EXACTLY ARE GOALS?

At the risk of down-playing its power, a goal is simply something you would like to do or accomplish! This means every time you set out to accomplish a task, you have set a goal. Every time you reach a predetermined target, you have met your goal.

Most individuals are quite successful at attaining goals which they have worked into their daily routine. Without even thinking about it they easily commit to maintaining their employment, house, car, and self. For instance, a person who wants to keep her job sets daily goals to be at work on time, dress appropriately, and put in a good day's work. Where people begin experiencing difficulty with setting and attaining goals is when fulfilling their ambitions becomes more than routine. When one has to stretch or alter one's life-style to get what one wants, one's commitment level sometimes sadly diminishes and the goals are often abandoned. With proper planning and preparation, everyone can learn how to work larger goals comfortably into their lives. Of course, there will be sacrifices and changes; however, with the right skills, attitude, and commitment, any sized goal can be attained!

GOALS GIVE DIRECTION

Goals work because they give you direction and specific targets. You have probably heard it said that a person without a goal is like a ship without a rudder, going around and around, never reaching any destination. In other words, without specific goals, one loses control and direction of one's life and instead, leaves chance and fate at the helm of one's destiny. Conversely, by setting and planning the attainment of your aspirations, you become the master of your own fortune.

Goals also act as the impetus for reaching your destiny. When someone is excited about reaching an objective, she will move mountains to attain it. Suddenly, instead of making excuses about not having enough time to accomplish a particular task, she makes the time. Instead of feeling overwhelmed and overworked, she feels invigorated and fortunate. A "turned on" goal setter has enormous power.

Not too long ago, one of our managers called me for help. She was planning a family vacation and two weeks before she was scheduled to leave she was confronted with an unexpected expense that completely drained her holiday fund. Distraught at the prospect of having to cancel her children's vacation, she was desperately seeking solutions to her financial problem.

To me the answer to this manager's dilemma was simple. She was already committed to her goal so I knew she could accomplish the impossible. As she was a very capable salesperson, all she needed to do was stop panicking and go to work.

I asked her how many bookings she had scheduled and she told me that because she wanted to spend the summer with her children, she had let her bookings run dry. I asked her how much money she needed and she told me that truly to enjoy her vacation she would need $1,000. I then asked her how much profit she usually generated from a social and she answered that she generally made over $100.

This manager now had the plan to reach her goal. What she needed to do was hold ten socials over the next two weeks and she would have her vacation money. Two days later, I received another phone call from her. This time she was excited and confident because she had already booked seven socials and had sold $200 worth of products through individual presentations. I didn't hear from her again until she came back from her vacation.

GOALS ARE YOUR BUSINESS PLAN

Goals are an individual's business plan! Can you imagine starting a business without a business plan? I can't! Furthermore, I'm certain that if your business required a loan from the bank, they would insist on a well-prepared financial plan. The bank would want to know how much money you expected to make, how you planned to secure the loan, what your cash flow projections were, and at what rate you anticipated being able to repay the loan.

North America operates on capitalist systems where goods and services are exchanged on a monetary basis. In our free market system, you are your own business. Your personal attributes and services determine the salary you secure. In other words, your ability to do physical work, level of intelligence, knowledge, and personality are all taken into consideration in determining your market value. Realizing that, in effect, you are your own business should help you to see the value of having a plan for your future!

WHY SOME PEOPLE DON'T SET GOALS

Knowing that goals are effective directional tools, one has to wonder why everyone doesn't set goals? Over the years I have asked this question 1,000 times. The reasons I am given are as varied as the people who deliver them. In reality, though, lack of desire and fear are the two underlying reasons why people don't set goals.

Lack of desire is at the root of excuses such as: "I don't know what I want," "I like my life the way it is," "I don't have enough time," "I already have too many commitments and responsibilities," and "If I make more money, the government will take it anyway." I have learned that it is virtually impossible to inspire desire in another person. As ambition comes from within, until you identify a reason to strive for a better future, you will remain exactly where you are in life.

Fear forms the basis of all of the following statements: "I would like to go after my dreams...but I don't know how...but I don't know if I have the ability...but I'm too old...but I don't have enough money...but what if I fail...." The cure for fear, of course, is action. With a little encouragement, and by setting and achieving first smaller, then progressively larger goals, anyone can gain the confidence and knowledge to achieve her life ambitions.

GOALS COME IN ALL SHAPES AND SIZES

As individual as the people who set them, goals can be aimed at financial or personal growth gains, and can range from a promotion at work, to learning how to ice skate, to accumulating millions of dollars. Financial goals target an increase in income in a specified period of time and are often tied to the attainment of an object such as a house, a new car, clothing, sending a child to college, a retirement nest egg, or an exotic vacation. Deciding to quit smoking, exercise more, increase knowledge in a particular area, or spend more time with your family are all personal growth goals. What distinguishes a financial goal from a personal goal is that the latter is not necessarily tied to a dollar value gain.

Financial goals and personal goals can be combined. A goal to enter or move up in management, or to complete a university degree, can be both personal and financial. Here the goal setter could be seeking an increase in knowledge, which is a personal growth goal, as well as an increase in income, which is a financial goal.

GOALS SHOULD BE BITE-SIZED!

Small, short-term goals, like cleaning the house and making it to work on time, are easily attained. Medium-sized goals, such as taking an evening course or increasing your monthly sales target, require more concentration and resolve. Larger goals to increase your annual income, obtain a university education, or save a down-payment for a house require a significantly higher commitment and effort. All goals, though, are quite attainable provided they are broken down into smaller bite-sized pieces.

Earlier we talked about the fact that most people are successful at attaining goals which they have worked into their daily regime. For instance, we don't question whether or not we should brush our teeth! In keeping with our overall goal to keep our teeth and close companions, we brush our teeth faithfully. Medium- and large-sized goals should be treated in the same manner! To tackle a larger or medium-sized goal, simply break it into yearly, monthly, weekly, and daily bite-sized pieces. Next, work your daily goals into your general routine, and you are on your way! Sound simple? It is! In fact, breaking your goals into daily targets is the key to getting everything you want from life.

TIPS ABOUT GOAL SETTING

To attain a goal, you must be very clear as to: what you want, why you want it, and when and how you are going to achieve it. Vague goals such as "I'd like to be in management," or "I'd like to earn more money," are too general. Why do you want to be in management? Why do you want more money? How much money do you want? When do you want it? What are the individual steps involved in attaining your goal?

To be effective, goals must be linked to time frames. A goal without a time frame is a wish. Wishes seldom come true unless you give them the attention they deserve. When planning a goal, be specific as to how much time you anticipate you will need to attain it. How much time you will need depends on many things including the size of your goal, your current circumstances, and the degree of commitment and time you are willing to devote. Be honest with yourself and remember the following two rules: 1) a given task will expand to fill the time allotted, and 2) goals that cause you to stretch too far will discourage you. When attaching your goals to time frames, allow neither too little nor too much time; instead, find the happy medium!

Goals should be reviewed periodically. Your plan to achieve your goal is also your success measuring stick. If you plan to save $10,000 this year and halfway through the year you are only one-quarter of the way to your goal, it will be up to you to determine the final outcome. Do you increase your work to increase your earnings in the later half of the year, or do you down-size your goal? The choice is yours!

Although you should commit to your goals as though they were carved in stone, they are not unalterable. Your goals may change as you grow and prosper. For instance, someone might enroll in college with the intention of becoming an economist. Once in school her focus might change and she might decide to become a lawyer. However, had she never set out to become an economist, she may never have discovered her ambition to enter the legal profession. Changing your goals is quite acceptable provided you do not alter your ambitions simply because the road becomes challenging.

When it is apparent that you need to acquire new skills or knowledge in order to obtain a goal, simply work this vital step into your long-term plan. Don't abandon your goal because you need to detour or delay your outcome; instead, include preparation time when mapping your road to success. For instance, if you would like to become a manager with your company but do not know the first thing about conducting recruiting interviews, holding meetings, and motivating others, then take the time to learn the skills you lack. Ask your own manager for help. Read books on management, motivating others, and administering meetings. In addition, start practicing what you are learning by participating in your company's weekly success meetings and holding interviews with potential team members. In time, you will acquire the skills necessary to obtain your goal!

Under, over, or through...
Obstacles can be overcome.

THE OBSTACLE COURSE OF GOAL SETTING

All goals risk being met with obstacles and challenges. Everyone, no matter what they may tell you, has good days and less-than-good days. Truly motivated individuals know that obstacles do not alter goals—the goal setter does! This means that *you* hold the power to overcome challenges that come your way and successfully attain your goal.

In the pursuit of any targeted outcome you may be faced with unforeseen delays or unwanted circumstances. Regardless, should your goal become blocked, you have the choice to find out why it is impeded, do what is necessary to get back on track, and then continue with your original commitment and enthusiasm. Once you are better equipped, you will succeed. For instance, if you were on a trip and you got lost, you would not abandon your vacation; instead, you would seek direction and continue. In spite of the delay, you would reach your destination and enjoy your trip. Remember, the old cliche, "Where there is a will, there is a way," holds true in the pursuit of all dreams.

DON'T JUST "TRY"!

Whenever a Camelion consultant shares one of her goals with me, I always state my belief in her ability to achieve her target. My conviction is a result of the fact that, as do all good direct sales companies, Camelion consultants and managers have everything in their favor. As individuals they are intelligent, warm, and energetic, plus they are equipped with superior products, training, and support. Therefore, I know that with the right attitude and commitment, they can do anything they decide to do!

Quite often, my confirmation of belief in a consultant is met with the response, "I'll try!" When I hear this response, every warning system in my mind becomes alert because "I'll try!" generally translates into, "I don't know if I can do it!" Unfortunately, when someone is not totally convinced of her ability to achieve an end, she will not likely do the required work. People do not give their undivided energy to something they are not certain they will be able to attain.

To succeed you must believe you will succeed. When you are uncertain of your ability to attain a goal successfully and find yourself thinking such things as, "I will try," make a conscious effort to replace your thoughts with "I will succeed!" or "I can do it!" Be alert for your own self-doubting attitudes and defeat them before they defeat you.

CORRECTING GOAL BLOCKERS

There is a secret place where you can locate and cure the most powerful goal blockers in the universe. It is also the very first place to look for solutions should your goals ever fall off the track to success. It is in your attitude. Many wise people have written valuable books on the power of a positive attitude, and for good reason! When you believe you can, you can. When you look for solutions, you will find them.

Too many people get lost in self-defeating thoughts and attitudes.

Instead of accepting where they are, and moving forward from there, many people choose to remain stuck in a rut! I remember a manager we once had who was not meeting her monthly team sales quota. I was curious to know why she was not reaching her goal and asked her what I could do to help. Her response was that all of her time was being spent taking care of her four children, preparing family meals, and tending her garden. I suggested that since all of her children were of school age, perhaps she could give them an increase in their allowances in exchange for their helping her care for the garden and with the preparation of family meals. Although she didn't have a reason as to why my idea wouldn't work, she told me she was convinced that it would not. I suddenly knew why she wasn't reaching her goal. She was stuck in her belief that she couldn't be a great mother as well as an effective manager. As she had great potential, I've always felt sad that she didn't continue with her Camelion management career. She could have had it all!

Everyone has one chance and opportunity at life on earth as we know it; you can either make the most of it, or waste it! People who let circumstances, disappointments, others, or excuses hold them back from getting exactly what they want are missing out on many gratifications to which they are entitled. They are not getting what they deserve because they are not demanding that they receive life's greatest pleasures! Demanding what is rightfully yours requires commitment and work. When you want something and you are willing to work for it, you shouldn't let anything stand in your way!

INVOLVE YOUR FAMILY

If you are married, involving your husband and children in your goals can be of paramount importance. After all, you will be taking time away from your family, and the fact that you have involved them in the planning stage of your ambitions will be greatly appreciated.

Let your kids and husband know what you are working toward. For instance, explain that you want to buy a new house or take a family vacation to Disneyland. If your children are young, post a picture of your goals on the refrigerator door. Well-displayed goals will remind your family of your aspirations and they will be less likely to be resentful of the times you are unavailable to them.

Many couples find that setting goals together is very rewarding financially and personally; however, if your spouse is not as committed to your goals as you are, simply ask him to support you in the pursuit of your dreams. Explain how important your goals are to you and that you would like to know that you have his good wishes.

YOU MUST BELIEVE!

If you can't decide on a long-term goal, don't worry. Decide on a short-term goal, and then after achieving it, decide on another short-term goal. As your accomplishments accumulate, your confidence will build and your goals will increase in magnitude. When you get to one hilltop, you can always see the next.

To attain any life ambition, you must believe you can reach your goal! Why does belief work? Because when you believe you can accomplish an end, you will be committed to your goal and do the work that is necessary with enthusiasm! When an obstacle comes your way, you will simply look for a way around it, over it, and when necessary, through it.

When I started with Mary Kay Cosmetics I set a goal to take their management training in Dallas, Texas as soon as I had met their prerequisite of six months in the sales field and a specified number of personal team members. Forty-eight hours prior to my targeted date, I was still two consultants short of the required number of personal recruits needed to attend management training. I could have simply waited one more month, but that would have meant that I couldn't attend training with my girl friend. Going to Dallas with my friend was very important to me because it was she who had encouraged me to strive for management with Mary Kay and she who kept telling me I could do it! I knew my girl friend would wait one more month if I asked her to, but I owed her more than that.

Twelve hours passed; I had not located any new team members and was quickly losing faith that I could reach my goal. I shared my fears with Terry, a friend of mine. Terry was in sales and was familiar with the pressures associated with a deadline. He also knew that I was losing faith. We were driving in his car when he came up with the solution to my problem. "I want you to scream at the top of your voice that you can do it!" was his expert advice. "Don't be silly," was my embarrassed response. "Say it! Say that you can do it!" he began shouting. "Okay, okay. Just keep your eyes on the road!" I answered. I was certain we would have a car accident! "I can do it," came my bashful cry. In an attempt to get my adrenaline flowing Terry continued shouting, "That's not good enough. Three times in a row, I want you to holler, 'I can do it!'" I began shouting and laughing, "I can do it! I can do it! I can do it!" The more I shouted, the more I laughed and the more I believed I could do it. And I did do it! In fact I ended up with four new team members in the remaining thirty-six hours.

Terry taught me the power of believing—a very important lesson I will never forget. When I let my goal seem impossible and got down in the dumps, I was quickly getting nowhere. When I accepted the challenge of the situation, started believing I could do it, and went to work with an abundance of enthusiasm, no one could say no to me. Why would they want to? I was excited, enthusiastic, and winning. Everyone wants to learn from and associate with winners. I had mastered one of the most valuable lessons of my life.

TEN STEPS TO SUCCESSFUL GOAL SETTING!

Now that you realize the inherent power of goal setting, it is time to get to work. The following exercise will help you identify and set your goals. Read the paragraph accompanying each step. Next, fill in your goals. Go ahead and write in this book so that when you review your progress, you will have your goals written next to the guidelines. In this way, should you fall off track, you'll be able to find the answers right next to your goals.

Step #1—Decide on Your Goals!

The first step in successful goal setting is to decide what you want to accomplish. Don't qualify or prioritize your goals yet; instead, let your imagination run wild as you list everything you would like to do, own, accomplish, and learn! Have fun with this part of the exercise and remember to dream big!

The things I would like to own are:

_____

_____

_____

_____

_____

The things I would like to learn are:

_____

_____

_____

_____

The things I would like to accomplish are:

_____

_____

_____

_____

The things I would like to do are:

_____

_____

_____

_____

Once you have finished listing your goals, divide them into categories according to: 1) how much time you believe you will need to accomplish them and 2) whether they are personal, financial, or combination goals. *Note:* Short-term goals should take less than one month to accomplish, medium-sized goals will take up to one year to accomplish, and long-term goals are just that!

Categorizing your goals will help you identify many dreams and ambitions you have abandoned. Later, we will look at prioritizing your goals and breaking them into smaller bite-sized pieces.

Remember Thomas Edison's wise words: "If we all did all the things we are capable of, we would literally astound ourselves!"

SAMPLE SHORT-TERM PERSONAL GOALS	SAMPLE MEDIUM-TERM PERSONAL GOALS	SAMPLE LONG-TERM PERSONAL GOALS
Start exercising	Learn to sing	Take two months vacation per year
Get my teeth cleaned	Learn to play the guitar	Live in a warmer climate for six months each year
Take more personal time	Go to Europe	
A weekend vacation		

YOUR SHORT-TERM PERSONAL GOALS	YOUR MEDIUM-TERM PERSONAL GOALS	YOUR LONG-TERM PERSONAL GOALS
1.	1.	1.
2.	2.	2.
3.	3.	3.
4.	4.	4.
5.	5.	5.

SAMPLE SHORT-TERM FINANCIAL GOALS	SAMPLE MEDIUM-TERM FINANCIAL GOALS	SAMPLE LONG-TERM FINANCIAL GOALS
Buy a new outfit for a special occasion	Buy a new car	Save for a house down-payment
	Increase my annual income by $10,000	

Make an extra $500 this month Read company manuals	Go to our company's annual seminar	Retire at age fifty
YOUR SHORT-TERM FINANCIAL GOALS	**YOUR MEDIUM-TERM FINANCIAL GOALS**	**YOUR LONG-TERM FINANCIAL GOALS**
1.	1.	1.
2.	2.	2.
3.	3.	3.
4.	4.	4.
5.	5.	5.
SAMPLE SHORT-TERM COMBINED GOALS	**SAMPLE MEDIUM-TERM COMBINED GOALS**	**SAMPLE LONG-TERM COMBINED GOALS**
Read a vocabulary building book Compile a personal attributes list	Take a computer course A promotion into management	Get a university degree Become manager of the year
YOUR SHORT-TERM COMBINED GOALS	**YOUR MEDIUM-TERM COMBINED GOALS**	**YOUR LONG-TERM COMBINED GOALS**
1.	1.	1.
2.	2.	2.
3.	3.	3.
4.	4.	4.
5.	5.	5.

Step #2—Prioritize

Once you have decided on your goals, you need to prioritize which ones you would like to achieve first. Goals are interrelated and achieving one is often dependent on another. For instance a goal to buy a house may necessitate an increase in purchasing power. An increase in purchasing power may require you to obtain a promotion at work, conduct a couple of extra socials per week in your business, etc.

To aid you in prioritizing your goals, next to each ambition you have previously listed, note the reasons why you want to achieve each goal. For instance, next to a goal for a house down-payment you might list your reasons as follows: I want to move to the country, I want to start a family and I will need more living space, I want to build more equity, and I want to have room for a garden. Next to a goal to take a computer course you might list: I want to be a writer and need to become more familiar with computers, and I would like to know more about computers for my own personal gratification.

Step #3—Timing

Deciding when you want to achieve each of your goals is as important as setting them in the first place. Simply saying, "I want to buy a motor home" is not good enough. When do you want to buy your motor home? What kind of motor home do you want to buy? How much money will you need? Remember to allow yourself adequate time to achieve each goal you set. You will get discouraged if you allow too little time to attain an end; if you give yourself more time than you need, procrastination may set in and cause you to abandon your goal.

Step #4—Develop a Plan

The decision made, now you need a plan to achieve each of your goals. For example, if you are goal setting to purchase a lakeside cabin, your plan will need to include: where you want your cabin to be, what specifications your cabin must meet, when you will purchase it, how much you are willing to pay, and how you intend to earn and save for the down-payment. Look at the following sample.

My number one medium-term financial goal: To purchase a lakeside cabin!

Why: I want somewhere to get away with my family throughout the year. I want somewhere to store my boat. I want a place where I can totally relax and forget about work. I want to increase my equity.

When: Within one year.

Where: Within fifty miles of the city, on a lake with good fishing and a beach.

What: My cabin must have two bedrooms, a fireplace, indoor plumbing, electricity, and a telephone.

Price range: $60,000 to $75,000.

Down-payment needed: $12,000 to $15,000!

How I will earn the down-payment: I will increase my direct sales business to earn the $15,000 I need for a down-payment. On an average I make $100 when I conduct a group showing. Dividing $15,000 by $100 means 150 group presentations. To do 150 group showings in a year I will need to do three more per week.

Step #5—Anticipating Obstacles

Selecting the goals you have prioritized, list all of the possible obstacles you might have to overcome, and where possible, solutions for overcoming them.

The following sample uses the above goal to save $12,000 to $15,000 within one year for a down-payment for a lakeside cabin.

POSSIBLE OBSTACLES	POSSIBLE SOLUTIONS
My husband might not like the fact that I am out most evenings.	Do one daytime and one evening group demonstration per week. Replace the other group presentation with five individual presentations per week!
Some of my hostesses might postpone their group demonstrations.	Replace every postponement with five individual presentations!

Step #6—Commit to Your Goals

I talked earlier about the importance of committing to your goals. Committing to your goals will require some sacrifices which may mean you have to forego some of your favorite activities. For instance, you may have less time to spend with your family. You might to have to cancel or change the time of your exercise classes. You might have to spend Saturday working at your goal instead of shopping with a friend, and the list goes on. When you are developing a plan to achieve a particular ambition, make certain you are honest with yourself as to the sacrifices or changes you will have to make. Ask yourself if you are willing to make these changes. If you are not, then you are not committed to your goal. If you are not committed to your goal, you will not achieve it!

Step #7—Put it on Paper

To help you focus, your goals and success plan must be committed to paper. Once you have documented your goals, position them where you will see them at various times throughout the day. Post your goals by your bed, on the bathroom mirror, on the sun visor of your car, in your datebook, on the fridge, or anywhere else where you will continually be reminded of your targets.

Be creative when posting your goals. For instance, color your posters and include pictures. If your goal is to get back into a size ten dress, keep a picture of a woman in a size ten dress on your refrigerator. If you were once a size ten, find pictures of yourself at that weight and post them all over the house! For those of you who are setting goals for material gains, post pictures of the things you want. If you have set a goal for a particular automobile, shop around until you find the exact car you want, including color and detailing. Then have your picture taken in the car of your dreams. Locating the exact automobile you want will help you determine how much you need to earn and save too!

Step #8—Get a Support Person

Once you have committed to a goal, share your goal with someone who is as motivated as you are and who supports you in your life endeavors. Ask that individual to be your support person. Be specific as to what you need from him or her. If you lack confidence, ask him or her to remind you continually of your strengths and your ability to achieve your goals.

When I was first starting in direct sales, I lacked many things. I didn't know how to sell. I was shy and had little self-confidence. One of my very best sources of support was a close family friend. Whenever I would become scared or discouraged, he would say, "If anyone can do it, you can!" I gained an enormous amount of courage from this fellow's belief in my capabilities. Although we no longer live in the same city, whenever I am feeling overwhelmed or confused, I still find strength in my friend's words of encouragement.

Step #9—Believe

Even the most brilliant success plan will be lost if you do not believe you can achieve your goal. I cannot even begin to count the times I have heard one of the following statements: "I knew I could do it!" and the antithesis, "I knew I'd never do it!" It is not too difficult to understand why each statement came to be. The person who knew she could do it accomplished her goal! The person who knew she would never do it probably did not do the work and give the commitment required to achieve her goal. Which person are you?

In Las Vegas and Reno the slot machines have a cute message to people they have just beaten. The message is, "No Pain...No Gain!" Although you may not find this humorous when the machine has just taken the last token in your bucket, there is great wisdom in the saying. Everything worth having requires some sacrifice and some pain. If you aren't willing to pay the price, you will limit yourself in what you are able to achieve. Growth is painful! Learning, as rewarding as it is, can be painful! The road to attaining your dreams and ambitions will have some difficult bumps and curves too. I can assure you, though, once your goals are realized, you will forget the pain!

Step #10—Work!

Once you have developed your success plan, work your plan. Sound too easy? It won't all be easy and circumstances may temporarily block your path. Sickness, unexpected pregnancies, family emergencies, household moves, increased responsibilities, etc. may necessitate a detour or delay in the attainment of your goal. Whether you let happenings stop you or decide to succeed in spite of what comes your way is your choice. It is a fact that your attitude will determine how you will handle obstacles in your path to success! Keep a positive, success-oriented attitude and you will win every time. You might get off schedule for a while, but you will win just the same!

CHAPTER SUMMARY

• A goal is simply something you would like to do or accomplish.

• Goals work because they give you direction and the impetus to attain an end.

• Goals come in all shapes and sizes, should be broken into bite-sized pieces, should be specific not general, must be linked to time frames in order to be effective, and should be reviewed and your progress measured.

- To attain any goal you must believe you can achieve it.
- Your attitude directly affects your ability to achieve your goals.
- The ten steps to successful goal setting are:
    1) Decide on your goals,
    2) Prioritize,
    3) Decide when you want each of your goals realized,
    4) Develop a plan,
    5) List the possible obstacles that may interfere with your ability to attain your goals,
    6) Commit to your goals,
    7) Put it on paper,
    8) Get a support person,
    9) Believe, and
    10) Work!

DIARY TO SUCCESS

CHAPTER TEN

Time Management Equals Business Management

The major keys to well-managed time are commitment, prioritization, planning, organization, and concentration. You must be aware of and committed to your priorities, and what sacrifices you will make in one area to accomplish your goal in another. Of course, by planning, concentrating, and organizing, all areas of your life can prosper!

COMMITMENT IS FULFILLMENT!

One only has to think of the numerous documented cases of superhuman strength both men and women have displayed to save a loved one's life to know that people are capable of incredible feats. It is a fact that we do not use our minds or our bodies to their full potential. The question is why not?

Although they are not completely contented, maybe even dissatisfied, many individuals settle for what they believe is their fate. Instead of demanding and working toward a more rewarding existence, they count their blessings for the fortune they have attained. It is true that as North Americans we are very lucky to have relatively easy lives where our essential needs for shelter and food are met. In fact, most of us survive rather well on a mere eight hours of work per day. It is this very comfort that causes some people to stagnate and not pursue their ambitions.

Changing a habit of complacency requires listening to your heart, mind, and soul and then committing to the fulfillment of your awakened desires and dreams. Commitment fuels your inner power and is a gift only you can give to yourself. How many times have you heard someone say, "When she decides to do it, she will!"? In other words, when someone commits to a goal, she is almost certain to succeed. The successful attainment of any objective, no matter how large or small, is truly a matter of pledging your total abilities and efforts to its attainment.

Belief in yourself and desire are important components of commitment. You will not commit to a goal you do not believe you have the abilities to achieve. And, if you lack desire, you will be void of much of the energy required to attain your goal. When you are plagued by nagging doubts about what you want or your ability to achieve an end, you will undoubtedly abandon your dream before it is realized.

As discussed in the previous chapter, taking the time to set and prioritize your goals is the easiest way to uncover your true ambitions; commitment is the surest way to realize them!

PLAN AHEAD AND GET ORGANIZED!

Getting organized requires forethought, effort, and an awareness of time-wasting habits that are stealing your energy. Regardless of your past habits, becoming organized is within your capabilities. Generally, disorganization is a matter of laziness or poor planning. As you read the following, stop and think about each point and how you can improve your organizational practices.

Maintain a tidy workplace! Keep your workplace neat and tidy. A messy desk is distracting and disturbing. No one can be expected to concentrate on the task at hand when mounds of papers, dirty coffee cups, and leftover candy wrappers are cluttering her space and her mind.

Establish a simple filing system! Set up a filing system and keep it simple. If you are working from a table, then purchase cardboard filing boxes in which to store your papers. You will also need file holders which are inexpensive and will save you from hours of searching for papers that you thought "were right here!" As soon as you are finished working with a paper, file it. As soon as you are finished working on a particular file, put it back in the drawer or box.

Deal with correspondence immediately! Buy or design stacking trays for incoming and outgoing mail. When you open your mail, be prepared to answer your letters and pay your bills. In fact, don't even open mail you are not prepared to deal with instantly. If you do not have the money to pay a particular bill, write the check and get it ready to go so that when you do have the funds, all you need to do is drop it in the mail. Whenever possible, answer inquiries by telephone, not mail; letter writing uses far more valuable time than a quick phone call.

Purchase office supplies! Purchase office supplies necessary for running an efficient business including: pens and pencils; a ruler; a highlighting pen; a note pad, datebook, address book and car mileage booklet; paper clips; file holders; a stapler and staples; stamps and envelopes; a brief-case; a rubber stamp with your name, address, and phone number (re-peatedly writing your name on receipt books and envelopes is a waste of valuable time); a calculator; a desk; and a weekly planning calendar.

Establish an efficient and simple record-keeping system! In business, you are required to keep invoices or receipts for:

1) Merchandise you are purchasing for resale. (*Note:* Goods taken out of your inventory to be used by you should be recorded in your sales receipt book. It is up to you whether you charge yourself retail or whole-sale prices for goods taken for personal use; however, you must remit sales tax for these.)

2) Sales you have made and sales tax you have collected.

3) Expenses you incur while conducting business. As a general rule, expenses incurred as a result of conducting business may be allowable tax deductions and include: hostess incentive gifts and products given for promotional purposes; stationery; stamps; motivational seminars and books; long-distance business phone calls; business-related travel ex-penses including food and lodging; and your business's portion of au-tomobile repairs, gasoline purchases, insurance, and parking fees. (*Note:* When you have a room in your home designated solely for business purposes, a portion of your rent or mortgage interest, electricity fees, and heating costs may also be allowable tax deductions. Check with your accountant or bookkeeper for current guidelines regarding these.)

Don't wait until the end of your business year to organize your records. The easiest way I have found for keeping accurate monthly business records is to purchase three large manila envelopes in which to store: 1) product purchase invoices, 2) completed sales receipt books, and 3) receipts for business-related expenses. (Label your manila en-velopes accordingly.) At the end of each month, summarize all three categories and place your receipts and invoices in permanent files. Study the following summary of purchases, expenses, and sales to see how easy it is to keep your records updated monthly.

MONTHLY SALES AND EXPENSE SUMMARY FOR MAY

MONTHLY SALES (from your receipt books):

Total sales	$2,564.50
Tax collected	$ 153.87
Grand total	$2,718.37

MONTHLY EXPENSES

Office supplies:

Datebook	$ 24.99
Paper clips	$ 1.57
Stamps	$ 3.90
Pens	$ 9.00
Subtotal	$ 39.46

Miscellaneous expenses:

Long-distance telephone calls	$ 17.00
Motivational seminar	$ 25.00
Subtotal	$ 42.00

Promotional expenses:

Hostess gifts and incentives	$ 75.00
Goods given away	$ 10.00
Subtotal	$ 85.00

Transportation costs:
My automobile odometer reading
at the beginning of the month was 10,500 miles
at the end of the month was 13,000 miles
13,000 minus 10,500 equals 2,500 total mileage traveled for business
and personal use in the month of May.

According to my mileage booklet, the distance I travelled for business
was 500 miles. Dividing 2,500 by 500 makes 5. This means 1/5 of my
gasoline and maintenance costs are directly related to my business. My
total gasoline purchases were $90.00.

$90.00 divided by 5 = $ 18.00
Parking receipts for business = $ 10.00
Total business-related transportation expenses for May = $28.00

Grand total of business expenses for the month of May:

Office supplies	$ 39.46
Miscellaneous	$ 42.00
Promotion	$ 85.00
Transportation	$ 28.00
TOTAL	$194.46

INVENTORY AND STOCK PURCHASES

Inventory at end of last month (April 30)	$2,056.00
Purchases for the month	
(Totalled from invoices for goods purchased)	plus $1,950.00
Inventory at May 31	minus $2,723.75
The cost of wholesale goods	
purchased for May	equals $1,282.25

SUMMARY OF COST OF DOING BUSINESS
FOR THE MONTH OF MAY

Total sales for May	$2,564.50
Cost of wholesale goods purchased	minus $1,282.25
Total expenses for the month	minus $ 194.46
Profit for the month of May	equals $1,087.79

Provided your records are kept updated and organized, preparing your income tax at the end of the year will be easy. If you are like me, you will simply take your filed receipts, monthly sales/expense reports, and year-end inventory total to your bookkeeper. Provided that your records are well maintained, the charge for a bookkeeper or accountant will be minimal.

Maintain accurate client records! Keeping accurate and updated records for your clients is essential to an efficient business too. We covered client files in Chapter 7. Refer back to that chapter if you are uncertain as to how to establish and maintain client records properly.

Establish a work station! Regardless of whether you have an actual office in your home, you will need a space from which to operate your business. If at all possible, designate a table or desk as your work station. Your work station must be away from family traffic and definitely not in the living or family room. There are far too many distractions in a room where the family normally spends evenings and free time. Your work space must have a telephone and ideally will be somewhere where you can leave your office intact. If you have to relocate all of your office supplies and files every time you conduct business, you will be wasting time and energy.

Work with a datebook! Your datebook is absolutely your best friend when it comes to managing both a business and family. Review the section in Chapter 4 on how to use your datebook for organization and profits.

Keep your purse/briefcase well organized! Ladies, keep your purses organized. Purchase a wallet and/or change purse. Straighten up your credit cards, makeup, and keys. A cluttered, overstuffed handbag will make you feel disorganized.

Keep a well-arranged, clean briefcase. Briefcases have a habit of becoming the "catchall" for paperwork we do not want to file. Clean your briefcase out on a weekly basis and file everything accordingly.

Note: Carrying both a purse and a briefcase at one time is considered unprofessional.

Write it down! If it is worth remembering, it is worth writing down. When you are managing a business and personal life, there are always numerous things to do and remember. Make a practice of writing everything you want to recall in your datebook. Because we often think of things we want or need to do when we go to bed, it is a great idea to keep a pad of paper on your night table. You may also find it useful to keep a note pad in your car so that you can jot down your thoughts when you stop for a red light.

PLAN YOUR WAY TO THE TOP!

Purchase a weekly planning calendar to help organize your overall business and personal obligations. At the end of one week, plan the next. Remember to include all of your business obligations such as: weekly success meetings, customer service and booking phone calls, individual and group demonstrations, and record-keeping time. As well, schedule your personal activities and routine chores including: church and club activities, exercise classes, laundry and ironing, gardening, shopping and meal preparation time, and vacuuming. When you map out all of the things you must complete in a week, you will find the time to do everything you must do and you won't feel overwhelmed and anxious. To keep your family informed of next week's agenda, post a copy of your weekly planning sheet on your refrigerator.

Plan client product deliveries! Make a point of scheduling errands and deliveries in an organized fashion along a prearranged route. In other words, complete all personal and business tasks in one area of town, before moving on to the next. Driving back and forth wastes time, fuel, and energy. To save even more time, schedule client product deliveries to coincide with personal errands or sales appointments. For example, where appropriate, drop off a client's order on the way to the dry cleaners or the bank.

Do two things at once! When one task does not require your total concentration, do two things at once. For example, do your laundry during an evening you have reserved for client servicing or booking phone calls. You are home anyway, and you will welcome the break from your phone calls when you stop to change laundry loads. When you are driving your car or preparing meals, listen to sales training or motivational tapes. When cooking, make a habit of preparing a double batch; serve one meal on the day it is cooked and freeze the other for a week down the road.

Don't put off until later what you can do now! This is especially important when you are confronted with a task you do not want to do. Don't waste time and energy feeling guilty and pressured by a dreaded task when you could complete it in a fraction of the time you would otherwise spend avoiding it. In fact, you will enjoy your day much more if you make a habit of ridding yourself of unwanted obligations first thing in the morning.

Learn to ask for help and to delegate! It continually amazes me that some women who have worked in the home taking care of their families, and who have recently joined the work force or field of business, still feel obligated to complete all household duties themselves. As wonderful as it would be to be "Superwoman," no one is. You may be super and you may be a woman, but trying to be "Superwoman" will lead you toward: ill health, a short temper with your spouse and kids, and an overwhelming feeling that you are sinking. My advice to all would-be "Superwomen" is…forget it! You can't be all things to all people all of the time. Your circumstances have changed, and you must too. Talk with your husband and children and inform them of your desires to achieve your business goals as well as make certain their needs are met. Once they understand your desires and burdens, they will be more than willing to pitch in and do their share. Just having the kids peel potatoes for dinner will help. Teaching everyone how to put in a load of laundry will reduce your burden further. Anyone over the age of twelve can run a vacuum through the house. Being a great housekeeper and cook for your family is important, but even more important is having the energy and time to be an attentive mother and wife.

Hire a housekeeper! If you wish you had more time to dedicate to your business, hire a housekeeper. Housekeepers charge a lot less per hour than you earn by working an hour on your business. There are numerous reputable housecleaning agencies to choose from, so locating a good housekeeper shouldn't be too difficult. Before hiring someone, decide which duties you want performed. If keeping the house tidy isn't too difficult for you and your family, perhaps all you need is someone to clean the stove, fridge, floors, and bathtub once a week. Maybe you would like someone to do your family's washing and ironing or prepare meals. Whichever duties you want performed, hire someone who is willing and able to do those specific jobs.

WORK WITH A PRIORITY LIST!

Prioritizing your day is essential to well-managed time. Make a habit of referring to your datebook and weekly plan sheet daily, and then prioritizing all of the tasks that need to be done. Of course, your appointments must be handled at their scheduled times, but the rest of your day needs to be organized too! Limit your daily list of priorities to between five and seven tasks. Begin with your top priority and work your way down the list. If you run out of time to complete a task, transfer it to your list for the next day. Remember, to avoid worrying needlessly, don't save unpleasant tasks until the last minute.

A priority list works because it keeps you focused and goal oriented. The payoff for organizing your time well is increased efficiency and a more relaxed life-style! Be aware that time is more important than money. When you spend money you can always get more, but when you spend (waste) time, you can never get it back!

CONCENTRATION SAVES TIME

Whatever you are doing…work or play…concentrate 100 percent! Aside from combining a simple task such as laundry with phone calls, you cannot concentrate on two things at a time. In fact, when you try to give your attention to more than one thing at a time, you will end up feeling overwhelmed and frazzled, which will lead to decreased productivity. Instead, concentrate on the job at hand, totally forgetting about everything else until you have taken the task as far as you can! For instance, when you are working on a particular file, put all other files away. Do as much work as possible on the first file before you pick up a second. When paying bills, concentrate until you are done. The same rule applies when you are making client service or booking phone calls.

To increase your effectiveness, tackle difficult tasks during your peak energy times. For instance, if you think most clearly during the morning, schedule complicated duties for then.

If you are concerned that a particular task will take longer than the time you have allocated or that your total concentration might cause you to miss a second deadline, set an alarm clock to ring when you must shift your attention. In this way, you can concentrate on your task without worrying about your next obligation.

Concentrate when you are playing too. When you are out for an evening with your husband, don't spend your time feeling guilty about a phone call you need to make, or business records that need to be filed. He will sense you are preoccupied and resent the fact that you are not totally "there." The same is true when you are spending time with your friends and children. It is also true that you will begin to resent your business if you are always worrying and thinking about the work you want to complete. Learn to turn your business "on" and "off."

AVOID TIME-WASTING MONSTERS!

When you operate a business from your home, you must guard yourself from "time-wasting monsters." Potential time-wasting monsters include: friends who drop by for tea (after all you always had time to visit during the day before), personal phone calls during work time, and long-winded clients who would like to share their entire life history with you!

If you want others to respect your time, you must respect your time. Decide how many hours you will dedicate to your business and when you will work. A full-time business demands at least eight hours of work each day; a part-time business requires a minimum of two hours of daily effort. Once you have established a business schedule, inform your family and friends of your intentions. Let them know why your work time is important to you and ask them to support your endeavors. If your children are young, color code your weekly plan sheet and post it on the fridge. Tell them that Mommy needs time to do her business and that when she is in "pink" time that means she must be left alone to make phone calls or do paper work. You may find you receive a lot more cooperation if your weekly plan sheet includes scheduled time with your children. For instance, if "pink" time is followed by "blue" time, and "blue" time is story time, your children will understand that their time with you is only a short distance away.

Now, in spite of all of your efforts to inform everyone of your business goals and intentions, your commitment to your work schedule is likely to be tested. Your best friend may call in the middle of your workday and want to come over for coffee. This will be the true test of your respect for your own time. If you want a break when the call comes in, you may be tempted to have your friend over to visit. Before you make this mistake, realize that friends never pop by for a quick cup of coffee—they come for an hour or two and your business day will be over about the same time your coffee break finishes. Instead of extending the invitation to visit when a friend calls, say something such as, "I would love to have coffee with you; however, I have promised myself that I will work on my business at this time each day. I hope you understand. Why don't we schedule a time to get together when I am not working?" Provided that you are tactful and honest, your friend will understand and accept your commitment to your business.

The above principle also applies when a friend telephones and wants to chat with you during your scheduled work time. Here again, you are faced with asserting yourself and asking if you can call your friend back after work, or neglecting your commitment to your business.

Talkative clients can also take up valuable work time. An effective way to shorten a telephone call is to stop responding. In other words, let the caller run on without offering even an "uh huh," "yes," or "no"! The conversation will quickly come to an end.

An egg timer is a useful tool for helping you to control the duration of phone calls. Each time you pick up the telephone receiver, turn over your egg timer; once or twice through the timer, end the call.

What do you do when a friend or acquaintance magically appears at your door during your workday? You stand on the front porch or in the doorway and talk to her. As rude as this may seem, showing up unannounced is rude too. Be aware...once your visitor is in your home, she will be there for an hour or more.

Keeping control of and effectively managing your time is a skill which can be learned and perfected with practice. Once you have successfully mastered this art, you will literally astound yourself with all you are capable of doing!

CHAPTER SUMMARY

• The major keys to well-managed time are commitment, prioritization, planning, organization, and concentration.

• Changing a habit of complacency requires listening to your heart, mind, and soul and then committing to the fulfillment of your awakened desires and dreams.

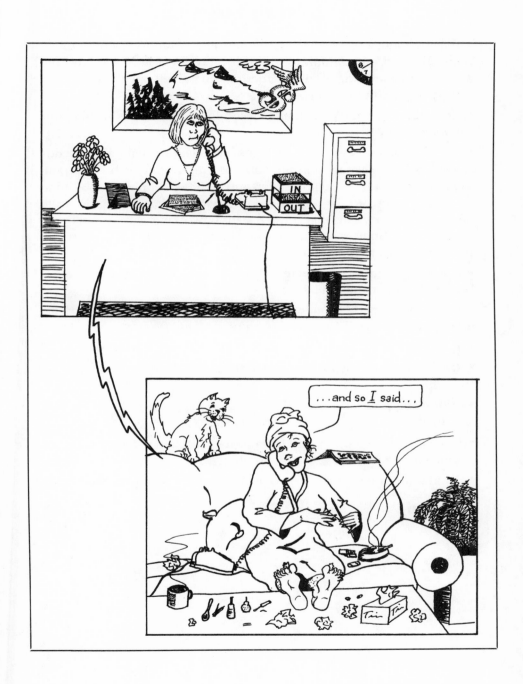

• Belief in yourself and desire are important components of commitment. You will not commit to a goal you do not believe you have the abilities to achieve and, if you lack desire, you will be void of much of the energy required to attain your goal.

• Regardless of your past habits, becoming organized is within your capabilities.

• In a direct sales business, being organized includes: maintaining a tidy workplace, establishing a simple filing system, dealing with correspondence immediately, purchasing appropriate office supplies, establishing an efficient and simple record-keeping system, maintaining accurate client records, establishing a work station, working with a datebook, keeping your briefcase in order, and writing down things that are important for you to remember.

• A weekly planning calendar will help you to organize your overall business and personal obligations.

• To save time, make a point of scheduling errands and product deliveries in an organized fashion along a prearranged route.

• To avoid wasting time, get into the habit of doing things *now!*

• Rather than trying to be a "Superwoman," learn to delegate and to ask for help.

• Prioritizing your day is essential to well-managed time; therefore, one should always work with a daily priority list.

• To receive maximum benefit from your efforts and to save time, learn to concentrate fully on what you are doing.

• If you want others to respect your time, you must respect your time.

DIARY TO SUCCESS

Recommended Reading List

MOTIVATION

Peale, Norman Vincent. *The Power of Positive Thinking*. New York: Fawcett, 1978.

Schuller, Robert H. *Tough Times Never Last, but Tough People Do!* Nashville: Thomas Nelson Publishers, 1983.

Ziglar, Zig. *Confessions of a Happy Christian*. Gretna, La.: Pelican Publishing Company, 1978.

Ziglar, Zig. *See You at the Top*. Gretna, La.: Pelican Publishing Company, 1974.

SELF-ESTEEM

Buscaglia, Leo, Ph.D. *Living, Loving & Learning*. New York: Ballantine Books, 1983.

Peck, M. Scott, M.D. *The Road Less Traveled*. New York: Simon & Schuster, 1978.

Whitfield, Charles L., M.D. *Healing the Child Within*. Deerfield Beach, Fla.: Health Communications Inc., 1987.

Index